The Art of Hosting

The Art of Hosting

The Complete Training Guide for
Waiters and Restaurant Hosts

Gerard A. Pollion

The Art of Hosting:
The Complete Training Guide for Waiters and Restaurant Hosts

Edited by Mark Jacobson
Illustrations by the author

Universal Publishers/uPUBLISH.com
USA • 2002

ISBN: 1-58112-613-1 (paperback)
1-58112-610-7 (ebook)

www.uPUBLISH.com/books/pollion.htm

Author's acknowledgements

To my renowned teachers Mr. Mazzetti and Mr. Guilleminot, at the Culinary Institute of Paris, France, for making me discover the European "Art of Hosting", including Enology, carving and tableside flambéing, my teachers and Maitre D's, including the Plaza Athénée and the Embassy of Great Britain in Paris, and many more.

For passing on their wine & spirits knowledge: Mr. Philippe De Nonancourt, CEO of Laurent Perrier Champagne, Épernay, France; Mr. Pierre Dupont, CEO of the Beaujolais/Côtes-du-rhône wine maker; Mr. Maurice Latour, CEO of the Bourgogne Latour wines; my friend and schoolmate, the late Mr. le Prince De Polignac, owner and producer of one of the oldest House of Cognac; the Bordeaux wine cellars' owners of Château Margaux, Cordier, and so much more.

My good friend Mark Jacobson, for help with editing and proofreading; and Mickel Madsen, Food & Beverage Manager, for his precious information on the American way of hosting, and so many other colleagues and supervisors that I had the pleasure to work with during my career.

And finally, and not the least, to my parents who showed me since my young age the best restaurants in France, my sister Michèle, Carine and Patrick, my beloved children whose lives were not always easy living in the family business, and

To you, who want to learn the Art of Hosting,

To all, my respectful thanks and gratitude.

TABLE OF CONTENTS

The Art of Hosting

The Art of Hosting

FOREWORD

All Gérard Pollion's experiences, from the time of his birth in La Ferté sous Jouarre, France, are totally reflected in the writing of this book. A practical, comprehensive guide to the art of hosting, it will allow any server to understand his or her profession by rediscovering the ancient tradition of hosting—using simple, easy to understand and logical guidelines. And every 'rule' is clearly explained, so you know why you're doing what you're doing, not just how. After all, it's easier to do something the correct way when you understand the logic behind it.

From the time that he observed the culinary activities of his mother as a child, Gérard has been fascinated by the art and practice of cooking and hosting. It was therefore not surprising that in 1961 he enrolled at the Université de Paris to study cooking with some of the greatest Master Chefs and Maîtres d'hôtel of France. His enthusiasm paid off in 1963 when he won the Diplôme d'Honneur Coupe Baptiste at the Maitre D' open tournament.

This book, therefore, devotes almost the same amount of attention to the total setting as the actual hosting or serving itself. This approach is very much in keeping with the tradition, philosophy and professional experiences Gérard has cultivated over many years in the restaurant industry as a chef, manager, maitre d' and owner.

Gérard Pollion is uniquely qualified to bring this information to you, and I genuinely hope that you get the most from what he has to share. I wish you the best of luck in your career in this wonderful industry!

Stanley H. Smith, PhD
Human Resources Academy Dean (Ret.)
South Illinois University, Carbonale, Illinois

The Art of Hosting

*The Best Dish in the World Served
in a Sloppy Way is a Disgrace*

INTRODUCTION

The goal of this book is simple: to teach you to be an outstanding host. Whether you wish to work in the finest of restaurants (and garner the greatest possible tips for excellent service) or a neighborhood bistro, you'll learn everything there is to know to host spectacular meals and banquets with professionalism and attention to detail.

Excellent hosting is not difficult, but it is an art that must be learned. And in my over 40 years in the restaurant industry, I have seen this art becoming more and more a 'lost' one as the years pass. In our hectic modern world, thorough (and correct!) training for servers in restaurants is very rare. This is what inspired me to write this guide for you. So you can work in the finest of restaurants (or any other restaurant that values good service) and hold your own, having complete knowledge of the proper way to serve your guests.

In this guide, I will cover every aspect of setting up, serving and clearing away food and wine. Using simple, concise descriptions, supported by an explanation of why you're doing things the way I describe, and clear illustrations and photos, you'll be able to quickly learn the proper techniques for hosting any guest.

Hosting is no more than using common sense in displaying all the tools needed to serve food & wine to your guests. Your goal should always be to host your guest just like you would like to be hosted: in a simple, elegant and undisturbed way. A total misconception that I hear too often is that "you must treat your guest as if he or she were your best friend" WRONG! Your guest is a temporary boss. The guest comes, orders and pays you. The guest, therefore, deserves respect, obedience and service.

The best host is a silent one: you don't feel his presence. He is as discreet as a shadow, using the art of efficient silence. Succeeding at this art means that the guest ignores your presence, as everything comes naturally, just like magic. The less your presence is noticed, the better the reward, and the better you will be remembered when it comes time to tip.

Everyone goes to a restaurant to have a good time, just like when you're going to a movie. You expect that it will be good and enjoyable. Just as a movie has many elements that are interwoven to make it good, so it is with a restaurant visit. The décor, ambiance, dining room set-up, lighting, music, choice of drinks and wine, food—even the perfect coffee must be just so in order to blend together to become the ultimate dining experience. And to crown all of this, smiling faces from the valet, hostess, bar and dining room staff. This must all be presented to the guest with efficiency, discretion and reserved politeness.

The proper hosting done this way will result in success, reward, recognition and repeat business. When the guest leaves happy, everybody has won. Let's begin our journey toward becoming a successful host.

A Lawyer has clients
A doctor has patients
A pilot has passengers
A mechanic has customers

A server has ... GUESTS

On Being a Server

Before you can be a server at the finest restaurant in town, you must first become an apprentice. This is a given in the restaurant industry. In fact, it takes years of practice to acquire the knowledge and skills necessary to perform with complete confidence and earn the respect only the best waiters receive.

In 1936, the first Hotel & Management Institution & Culinary Institute was created at rue Médéric in Paris, France, originally named "Ecole Hôtelière Jean Drouant". The primary goal of this institution was to alleviate the years of on-the-job training needed to become a professional in only one single field by giving three years of intense teaching that combined the theory with training and practice. This teaching included Dining room, Enology, Culinary, Accounting, two foreign languages (spoken fluently), Hotel and Management.

The advantage of this system is to give a total overview of all professions within the hotel/restaurant business. And later, to give a better understanding all the facets of this industry.

Once graduated, one was able to choose the branch of his/her choice and be able to enter and climb rapidly the echelons of that field. Six months after graduation, anyone could ask for a server's job in fine dining establishment, knowing in-depth tableside carving & flambéing, decanting and wine knowledge.

The Art of Hosting

In my own places in France, whoever applied for a job in the kitchen had to spend one full month in the dining room and vice-versa; this practice allowed my entire staff to better understand the difficulty of the other side, making the better able to perform their own function.

In North America, it seems that a great number of the wait staff lack the basic knowledge necessary to work in the restaurants where the money is. The goal of this book is to teach you just that, without having to spend thousands of dollars and several years on a formal education in Europe.

The Wait Staff

No one starts in this industry as a Dining Room Manager! The restaurant business is a TEAM effort, where the higher level masters the lower one. Here are the duties that must be learned and the necessary steps to become one of the best:

- Bus Boy

This job is basically one of a handy man: performing the lowest duties while learning the restaurant and how it runs. During mealtime, the busboy's duty is to have the first contact with guests, bringing bread & its garnishes, clearing emptied plates and carrying them to the dishwasher. It requires discipline, obedience, total devotion and service without question.

- Food Runner

He or she must first have a full knowledge of all dishes and their presentation and the station locations. Picks up food in the kitchen, makes sure there are cold plates for cold food and hot plates for hot food, covers hot food plates with a cover. Carries food on a tray to the proper table, sets it on a tray jack that is carried at the same time and advises the Captain of its arrival.

- Server

The waiter's job is to wait for the food to arrive, and then serve it. He or she also assists the Captain in all duties and situations.

- Captain

  Takes the food and drink orders, including wine orders when a wine steward is not available. He or she also performs tableside carving & flambéing and stays in his station at all times to see to the guests' needs.

- Bartender

  Serves all drinks to bar guests. The only wait staff member that is allowed to be social (in a respectful way) with guests.

- Wine Steward

  A former Captain who has spent years of studying Enology (the scientific study of wine). In charge of the cellar and "Cave du jour". Advise guests on how to properly marry their food with wines, takes wine order, does the decanting and serves the wines and after dinner drinks.

- Host/Hostess

  In charge of the lobby cleanliness, updates daily the reservation book, takes telephone reservations, welcomes guests and conducts them to the table. Brings menus (if not already on the table), informs the Captain of guest's specific information or requests (the paying guest, birthday, etc.) and thanks guests on their departure.
  Note: Hosts and Hostesses should always be dressed appropriately and be well groomed, with no jewelry, perfume or cologne.

- Maitre D'

> In charge of the entire dining room. Performs scheduling, oversees the guests' tables. Visits guests' tables and inquires about their satisfaction or any problems that they may not feel comfortable telling their Captain.

- Dining Room Manager

> Often combined with the Maitre D' position; the Dining Room Manager fills out the necessary paperwork, including shift and daily reports, and reconciles bartender and dining room cash register tills. Establishes wait staff station assignments. Issues menus, specials menus, cocktails, coffees, cocktail coffees, after diner drinks and wine list. Arranges special parties, banquets and buffets. Brings more business to the restaurant by working with the Public Relations firms, wine suppliers and others. Orders any equipment needed in the dining room.
>
> The Dining Room Manager is in charge of the entire restaurant operation, while having permanent contact with the Chef. Finally, the Dining Room Manager reports to the General Management and ownership.

The Art of Hosting

CHAPTER 1

Dining Room Set-up

This chapter will show you how to set up a dining room, taking it from an empty space to an arrangement of tables for a comfortable guest seating in the finest of restaurants. Since different styles of restaurants have different requirements, we'll talk about how the dining room setup can be tailored in each case.

Positioning Tables

Positioning Chairs

Booth Options & Shapes

Numbering Tables

Guest Positions

Floor Plan

Dressing the Table

Server's Stations

POSITIONING TABLES

The main concern when it comes to a dining room is the seating capacity. There are basic rules, depending on the type of restaurant: upscale, fine dining, ethnic, family, fast food, banquet, or anywhere in between. The owner's investment is therefore a major component of your irrevocable decision.

Below are the recommended dining room floor plans. Variations can be made based on this framework. Always keep the comfort of your future guests in mind—décor, ambiance and music all play a part. The more expensive your prices will be, the more comfort you can afford to give and the less seating capacity you will have!

Arrange the table setting according to the pole of attraction inside the dining room (fountain or other example, or outside (ocean view, scenery, etc). While inside your restaurant, every one of your guests wants to have the best table, so strive to place all tables around the focal point so that everyone can have a good view of it. If your restaurant has an outside view, place your table rows on steps (which is excellent, but expensive!), or place your tables in the shape of "wolves teeth" in order to squeeze additional tables.

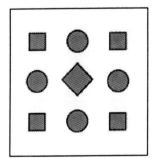

HARMONY

The visual harmony of the entire dining room is your main concern. In order to be pleasant to the eye, you must avoid monotony. Therefore: *always alternate square and round tables.*

PRIVACY

Keep in mind that guests like a maximum of privacy. Whenever possible, place a large plant or a thin wall divider between two tables to create 'alcoves'. When placing a table, always remember to avoid facing a chair face to face with another chair from another close table. If guests want to sit next to each other, have the same chair position from the other table.

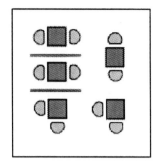

COMFORT

• Leave a minimum of 5 feet between each table to allow fluid service and guest privacy.

• Leave room around tables for tray-jacks and service.

• Never place tables at the back of the room or near the kitchen, service door, heavy traffic or bar areas.

• Avoid placing tables next to sources of noise (bar, live entertainment, etc.)

POSITIONING CHAIRS

PRIVACY: Positioning chairs & armchairs properly means keeping in mind the maximum privacy that the guests always request: a date, a business occasion, a family reunion, etc.

COMFORT As common sense dictates, the use of armchairs is always preferable for round tables and square tables that seat 2 or 4 persons. For long tables, regular chairs are recommended as they use less space in between each guest.

THE ENEMY The walls: they are the chair-positioning enemy. Here are some simple chair DOs & DON'Ts:

DO
DON'T

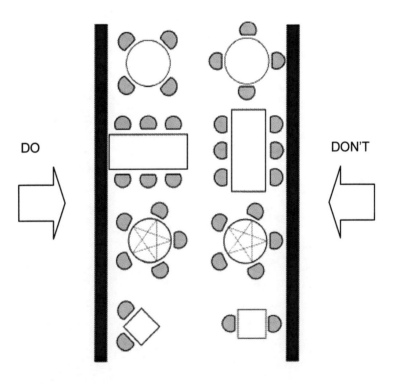

BOOTH OPTIONS & SHAPES

Although initially more expensive than chairs, the investment in booths is worth it, as more people can be seated in less space. Using a banquette allows the tables to be against each other with limited, but acceptable privacy for the guests. Keep in mind that a booth layout is a fixed set-up for a limited number of people and cannot be extended as with tables.

BRASSERIE TYPE

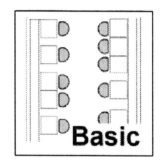

Originated in France, this set-up accommodates a large seating capacity with comfort as guests are seated closer to each other (extra room in between tables is eliminated).
The "Straight line" is the basic layout, allowing the seating of deuces (2 persons) at one table, and more people by putting additional tables against one another.
The disadvantage is that one person is seated to a comfortable booth (generally the lady) and the other on a chair facing the wall!

THE "E" SHAPE

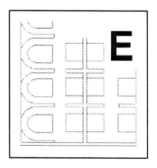

This shape is more economical to build than the "S" (below), but has less privacy, since one table faces the other. Therefore it has to be seriously considered before building it; it is not recommended if the majority of your clientele will be business people (or, even more, with romantic couples on dates!).

11

THE "S" SHAPE

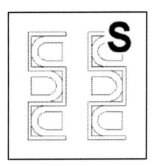

This is certainly the most expensive booth shape to build than the previous ones, but it is the best of the booth shape options: each booth has complete privacy; no other table (or guest) is directly facing another table.

Its shortcoming is that it only seats a limited number of people (maximum 4 to 5 comfortably).

NUMBERING TABLES

This is an crucial step that does not allow any room for error: each table must be immediately recognized not only by the entire dining room staff, but also by the kitchen in order to allocate the food to the proper guests' table and prepare all the dishes for that particular table.

Once established, the numbering system **cannot** be changed in the future; therefore it must not allow any confusion and be very simply recognized by anyone.

SINGLE ROOM

The shape of a dining room varies from one place to the other. The basic rule is to number the left first table at the guest entrance door with number 1 (*never use 0 or 13*) and go clockwise around the room.

In a row-type layout, it is preferred to start numbering from the table closest to the kitchen, starting with 11 and up for the first row, then 21 to the second row, and so on.

SEVERAL ROOMS

Each room should starting numbering with a different thee-digit number: 101 and on for the first room, 201 for the second, and so on.

If the rooms have different levels, or front and a garden setting, etc. use the same system.

Differentiation creates immediate recognition and avoids damaging mistakes, like delivering food to the wrong table!

ROOM ADDITION

A restaurant usually and originally starts with one dining room (numbered from Table #1, also called the "Ace") With success, other rooms may be added. As you cannot change the original first room numbers, start with the number 201 (the 201 meaning the first table of the second room), etc.

FINESSE

A small restaurant that I once visited in France had only a few tables. In keeping with its very sophisticated, dining and service, the owners named each table after of a different flower.

The hostess conveyed us to the "Orchid Table", where a vase of Orchids was placed. Too complicated for a large restaurant, but it gave a final touch to this exquisite and romantic place that I'll remember the rest of my life.

GUEST POSITIONS

To illustrate the reason and importance behind the guest's position system, just think about the following situation that unfortunately occurs too often.

The order was taken and now it's time to serve the food to the guests. How many times have you heard:

" ... and ... the filet-mignon medium-rare is for ... ?"
one guest answer and the filet-mignon is served to this guest, then another:
" ... the filet-mignon rare is for ... "

then the first guest realizes the mistake, and says:
" ... Oh no! the rare is for me ...! "
sometimes followed by
" ... I'm sorry ... "
making the guest guilty and uncomfortable, as it is the unprofessional server's mistake: the order was taken a while ago, but no one remembers who gets what!

As a consequence, the plates start moving around in total confusion.

To avoid such embarrassment, the guest's position system is primordial and must be uniform in the entire dining room and among the whole wait staff, as it allows anyone to be able to serve without mistake.

According to the layout of a dining room, it may vary from one establishment to the other and must be requested by any new wait staff. A good rule of thumb is to start the number one (1) at bottom left of a table when facing the main entrance of the dining room.

The numbering order is always clockwise.

FLOOR PLAN

Now that the tables are harmoniously positioned in the dining room, numbered properly (and permanently), and the guests' positions have been determined, it is time to make a floor plan.

The floor plan is the simple overview of the dining room that is posted at:

1. The Hostess/Maitre D's front desk to allocate table reservations, establish wait staff stations, and help to turn tables in sequence in order to optimize their profitability.
2. The dining room stations and wait staff kitchen service area, for easy and immediate table station recognition
3. The kitchen expediting station, for food runners to know where to deliver guests' food
4. The Chef's and Manager's offices, for dining room daily planning and special parties.

It should also include, for each table, the guests' seat number as shown below.

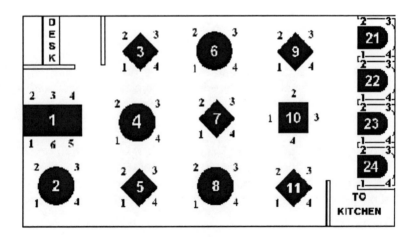

DRESSING THE TABLE

Look at a table like you would a bride:

- The lingerie protects and enhances the dress. The blanket (also called "felting") does the same with the raw table.

- The wedding dress is the tablecloth, the more fashioned the dress, the more elegant the tablecloth.

- The veil is small and adds beauty to the bride's ensemble. The veil on the table is a smaller tablecloth that adds beauty to the regular tablecloth.

- Like diamond jewelry and other accessories, the silverware, crystal glasses and show plates (large, often decorated plates that fill the empty space when setting the table) all enhance the table's appearance and add the finishing touches.

THE "LINGERIE": FELTING

Most tables have sharp angles, are rough and may have some defects. Therefore tables are covered with a *felting* (light 'blanket'), which is nailed or stapled on the underside of the table. Sound on the table will now be dampened and the edges will now be smoothed.

This is the classic and inexpensive way to dress a table. It's what makes the difference between a cafeteria table and an upscale restaurant table.

THE "DRESS": TABLECLOTH

Whatever the material, the tablecloth should be:
- Well ironed
- Placed right side up (with seams inside)
- Centered on the table, with each side hanging over by the same length, as shown below.

All the tablecloths in the dining room must be of the same length, to ensure harmony and give the room a uniform and polished appearance. When using a square tablecloth over a round table. *Each tablecloth corner must be in front of a table leg.*

THE "VEIL": TABLEMAT

This smaller tablecloth is placed on top of the tablecloth. Made of lace or the same material as the tablecloth, it protects the tablecloth from spills (so you don't necessarily have to replace the tablecloth after each guest).

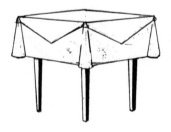

The hanging length should be no longer than half the length of the tablecloth and each corner in between the tablecloth corner.

The veil gives the final touch that really dresses up the table. All hanging veils in the dining room must be of the same length.

SERVER'S STATIONS

Stations are limited in number and are spread around the dining room. They are the dining room "warehouse" areas that contain all necessary equipment used by the wait staff during the course of the meal shift.

Each station must be fully stocked prior to the shift to avoid wasting time restocking during the shift. It should also remain spotless during the whole shift, regardless of whether it is in guests' view or not. Its content varies according to the type of restaurant and ethnic cuisine.

Here is what you'll typically find in a restaurant station and how it should be kept:

Computer Terminal	Clean & wiped before and after each shift.
Credit Card Dialing Equipment	
Credit Card Forms	Properly stacked in their box cover. Must have enough for the entire shift.
Pitchers	Iced tea and water pitchers are placed on a plate and covered with a napkin to avoid condensation on the countertop and avoid being slippery. Must be refilled regularly during the shift.
Marking Plate	A large plate covered by a folded napkin. All silverware that guests may need during the course of their meal, including steak knifes, are properly aligned inside a folded napkin. This silverware must be at constant levels during all shifts, and added when necessary

Silverware	All types of silverware to be used during the course of the shift, clean and properly aligned in groups. They are set on a rectangular tray or in a drawer (if available) and topped with a clean napkin (to be replaced after each shift).
Serving Silverware	Forks and spoons used as tongs. To be placed alternately: one fork, one spoon, etc. on a large plate, topped with a clean napkin.
Plates & Underliners	Each type and size on a separate pile. After each shift, they are covered with a clean napkin to avoid dirt deposits.
Salt / Pepper Shakers	Must be cleaned and refilled after each shift. Originally on the table, they are cleared before dessert is served.
Oil and Vinegar Bottles	To be cleared from the table, as soon they are not needed anymore. These bottles must be cleaned and refilled before each shift.
Cheese Grinder	Cleaned before each shift and refilled before the shift starts. They must be returned immediately after use, as they never stay on the guest's table.
After Dinner Mints	Served in the dining room with guest's check; they should be stored in a clean container.
Ashtrays	Cleaned, wiped and properly stacked.
Folded Napkins	Properly stacked in sufficient quantity to reset tables during the shift. When using rollups, it is a good idea to store them in a basket, away from dirt and spillage.

Serving Napkins	Clean, folded and properly stacked.
Menus	When not at the front desk (Hostess/ Maitre D' stand), they are kept in the station. Covers, too, must be perfectly cleaned and the inside checked after each guest's use and replaced immediately if necessary.
Dessert Menus	Same as above.
Coffee, Cocktail	Same as above, if separate from the dessert menu: same with Coffees and After Dessert and Dinner Drink Menus.
Check-Presenter	In good condition and spotless.
Small Trays	Covered with a clean napkin.

The Art of Hosting

CHAPTER 2

Table Set-up

Since the table is where guests will spend their entire dining experience, setting it up properly is the final touch that can make or break the entire dining experience. The table must be spotless. It must be elegant, but somewhat neutral, so the different food courses and wines can stand out and truly be appreciated.

As always, there are rules to follow that are just common sense.

Plates

Silverware

Glasses

Napkins

Miscellaneous

PLATES

One never imagines that we had to wait for centuries, even millennia, for the plate to appear on our tables. In the Middle Ages, a large slice of bread was set in front of each guest, so the juices from the meat would not run all over the table. The bread slices, full of protein, were then distributed to the poor waiting outside the castle.

Lord Sandwich put his meat in between these slices of bread— his hands were cleaner, so was the table! Until the Italian Renaissance, food was served in large serving dishes and the food was eaten by hand (its seems that the fast-food industry caused a rebirth of this primitive way of eating!)

It is always the wait staff's duty to make sure plates are spotless—not chipped and at the proper temperature (cold plate for cold dishes, hot plate for hot dishes) at the beginning of each shift. When dressed, filled and garnished by the kitchen crew, make sure that their rims are perfectly clean and spotless before bringing them to the dining room.

THE SHOW PLATE

The Show Plate or "Plate Charger" dresses the empty spot were plates will be set and protects the cleanliness of the tablecloth.

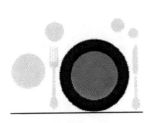

Place it exactly in the center where each guest will be seated, prior to the guests' arrival. It will stay until dessert is served. Position it even with the edge of the table rim, exactly opposite the Show Plate on the other side of the table. Don't forget that the rest of the glasses and silverware will go around its position.

If the Show Plates are unaligned, the whole table will be crooked!

24

BREAD PLATE

Too often neglected, this small plate is placed on the center-left of the Show Plate or where the larger plate will be placed (usually the entrée plate). It will receive the bread and butter, along with its own small knife. This plate is removed before crumbing the tablecloth and before dessert is served.

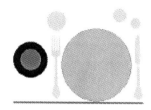

THE UNDERLINER

It must be topped with a doily and is a must for ALL plates that will carry food and any glasses with no stems, coffee cups/saucers etc. It limits accidental spillages around the plate, and gives a place to rest silverware in between their use.

THE OTHER PLATES

Used for dishes served during the entire course of the meal and placed on the Show Plate.

Location: Side garnishes, vegetables & starches plates are placed next to the bread plate, the sauceboat on the right of the plate with serving spoon going rightward for guest's easy handling.

Fingerbowl or wet napkin with lemon plate served after any dishes where hands are used (primarily Seafood) are placed on the left of the plate and removed immediately after the guest's hands are clean.

25

SILVERWARE

Some dishes require special silverware in order to be eaten properly and easily. Some are widely available, while others are sold in specialty shops and upscale department stores.

(Silver silverware must be polished once a week by the wait staff.)

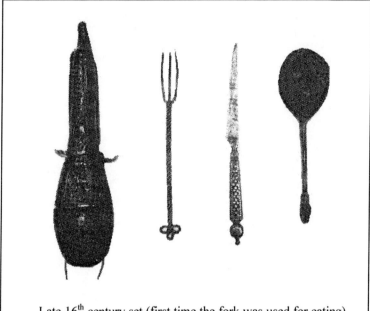

Late 16th century set (first time the fork was used for eating)
The silverware was personal. Each guest brought its own, bagged
in a leather poach (left)

The position of each piece of silverware is really just common sense (if you're right-handed). The silverware that is placed to the right of the guest's dinner plate is nearly always put at a 45^0 angle, to be immediately noticed by the guest and at an easy angle to be picked up and handled.

Here is an overview of all the silverware you will come across for the most common dishes in restaurants, along with their proper position on the table.

Dish	Utensil	Location	
SOUP	Soup spoon	Right	45^0 angle
ASIAN SOUP	Ceramic spoon	Right	45^0 angle
SALAD	Dessert fork	Left	Parallel to fork
	Dessert knife	Right	Parallel to knife
SHRIMP COCKTAIL	Small 3-teeth fork	Right	45^0 angle
CAVIAR	Caviar spoon	Right	45^0 angle
ESCARGOTS	Tong	Left	Parallel to large fork
	Small 2-teeth fork	Right	45^0 angle
OYSTERS on the half shell	Small 3-teeth fork	Right	45^0 angle
CLAMS on the half shell	Small 3-teeth fork	Right	45^0 angle
SEA URCHIN	Teaspoon	Right	45^0 angle
WINKLE	Pins picked in a cork	Right	Below white wine glass
LOBSTER	Nutcracker	Left	Parallel to large fork
	Small 2-teeth fork	Right	45^0 angle
PASTA	Large spoon	Left	Parallel to large fork
FISH	Fish knife	Right	Parallel to knife
	Fish fork	Left	Parallel to fork
STEAK	Steak Knife	Right	Replace the knife
FONDUE	Fondue fork	Right	Slightly angled
ASIAN DISHES	Chopsticks	Right	Replace the knife
CHEESE	Dessert knife	Right	Replace the knife
	Dessert fork	Left	Replace the fork
ICE CREAM	Dessert spoon	Right	Replace the knife
	Dessert fork	Left	Replace the fork
CAKE			
no sauce	Dessert spoon	Right	Replace the knife
with sauce	Dessert fork	Left	Replace the fork
SOUFFLE	Dessertspoon	Right	Replace the knife

GLASSES

Let's face it—everyone thinks they know their glasses: red wine, white wine, water, etc. That's it, right? Wrong. As an apprentice will soon discover, there is a large variety of glasses out there, each of which must be chosen according to the type of drink they will hold. Spend some time learning your glasses, as it generates sales (and increases your tips).

COCKTAIL GLASSES

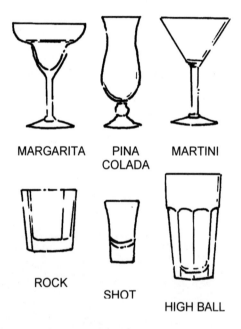

MARGARITA   PINA   MARTINI
              COLADA

ROCK

SHOT

HIGH BALL

A large variety of cocktail glasses are now on the market. They are *always* stocked at the bar, where the bartender uses them in making the ordered drinks.

In some restaurants, the captain, waiter or cocktail waitress has to present the glasses to the bartender in order to fill the order—another important reason to know your glasses and their use.

WINE GLASSES

BURGUNDY

WHITE WINE

BORDEAUX

SPARKLING

MOSEL / ALSACE

Each type of wine must be served in the appropriate glass:

- Chilled white wines are served in narrower, smaller glasses than red wines, since they are refilled more often with the chilled wine from the bottle.

- Room temperature red wines are served in wider-bodied glasses called *ballons*, which allow the wine's bouquet to expand in the glass. It is important to serve a good vintage wine in a large glass.

AFTER-DINNER GLASSES

SHERRY

SNIFTER
COGNAC
&
BRANDY

GRAPPA

CORDIAL

Only in upscale restaurants will you find an after-dinner drink cart. The cart is brought to the guests' table (where the appropriate glasses are stocked) where the captain/sommelier serves the after dinner drinks.

If they are not set on the after diner drink cart, after dinner glasses are stocked at the bar/service bar, where the bartender will fill the order using the appropriate glass.

WATER, ICED TEA & SODA GLASSES

Their shapes vary according to the class of the restaurant:

- A plastic glass is perfectly acceptable in a family-style restaurant. They keep costs down, since they are affordable and don't break easily.
- ☆ to ☆☆☆: A highball glass is recommended.
- ☆☆☆☆ to ☆☆☆☆☆: A white wine glass is mandatory.

WINE
GLASS

HIGHBALL

PLASTIC

Note: If a lemon slice is to be used (which is *not* recommended), it must be placed on a separate small plate (for stemware glass), on the underliner (for highball glass), or, eventually on the rim, but *never* inside the glass: this is the guest's choice, as lemon kills any wine that is drunk after and some food & sauces!

NAPKINS

There are several types of napkin, each having a specific purpose:

PAPER NAPKINS

Cocktail napkins: they are placed under drinks (when there is no tablecloth on the table). They can also be used in place of small-laced doily.

SERVICE NAPKINS

Used by wait staff for holding hot plates and to crumb the tablecloth (in place of the metallic curved bread crumber). Also used to cover trays.

FOLDED NAPKINS

Modern dinner napkins come in sizes ranging from 18 to 22 inches square. (*Ironically, it looks like we can put a man on the Moon, but are unable to find a real 'square' napkin!*)

Napkins must be lightly starched to be folded into interesting shapes. Linen or cotton napkins are the best to work with. There are hundreds ways to fold napkins, for the simplest to the more elaborated.

> (*The fan fold, so often seen in restaurants and clubs, is never used at home as its look has a tendency to be the focus of the dining room setting, overshadowing the décor of the household*).

In restaurants, choose a folding that matches the décor, ambiance of the dining room, but don't over-do it. For special parties, choose a folding that matches the occasion.

Below are a few examples done in European Courts, a few hundred years ago. Needless to say that the time and dexterity required a full crew whose only job was to fold napkins!

Place folded napkins in front of each guest (directly on the tablecloth if no show plates are available).

Always have handy black folded napkins (instead of the whites) to present a guest who wears dark pants or a skirt: this will avoid white lint on their black cloth).

ROLLUPS

Napkins are also used as "rollups" where silverware is wrapped-in.

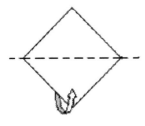

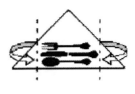

1.
Fold the napkin in a triangle,

2.
Place the silverware all facing the same direction,

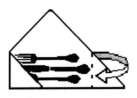

3.
Flip both side of the base of the triangle over the ends of the silverware,

4.
Roll the napkin from the base to the tip of the triangle.

Place the rollup on the right side, as the Menu will be placed in the front.

CHAPTER 3

Banquet Set-up

The purpose of a banquet is to assemble a large number of people for a special occasion. The set-up is usually discussed with the person who books the party, including the number of people at the table of honor, etc.

Depending on the style of the party, the number of guests and so on, the layout of the tables will change. On some occasions, the center of the room may be reserved for a dance floor or a centerpiece. The whole room must be set-up with harmony and elegance: banquets are special events after all!

Positioning Tables

Numbering Tables

Dressing the Tables

Positioning the Chairs

Seating Set-up

Plates

Silverware

Glasses

Miscellaneous

POSITIONING THE TABLES

The Banquet setting differs from the standard dining room setting, as its purpose is to seat a larger amount of people, while keeping the guests' comfort in mind. In order to achieve this, there are two basic set-ups, which can be adapted according to the event and the size of the room.

THE TABLES

- TYPE:

  Always use long tables (folding tables or others). Never use square tables.

- SIZE:

  They should all be the same height, but may vary in length, so glasses and plates will be level, etc.

- POSITION:

  Butt tables against each other to form single, long rows having the same length and forming a general design or shape.

THE "U" SHAPE

This shape is for a relatively limited number of people in a long, rectangular room.
- The table of honor is placed parallel to the narrower wall of the room and against it.
- Place the two other tables at 90^0 angles on each side of the edge of the table of honor.

THE COMB SHAPE

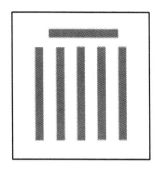

Also called the "rattle" shape, this table position differs from the "U" shape in that a large number of long tables are placed between the "U". This shape can accommodate a very large number of people.

Leave a 4-foot space between each branch of the comb and the table of honor to allow better circulation and service fluidity, and 7-foot space between each branch of the comb.

VARIATIONS

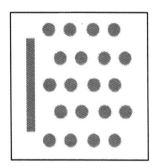

Sometimes a more intimate shape is desired, marrying the basic dining room set-up with the banquet set-up.

A long table seats the guests of honor, while large round tables that can sit 8 or more people are used to keep some type of intimacy while being part of the entire event.

NUMBERING TABLES

A banquet setting has a limited number of (large) tables that are numbered in many ways but easily recognizable *(letters are the most common)*.

A visible sign with its number is posted at the center of each table, usually part of the flower centerpiece arrangement.

In a restaurant dining room, table numbers are for the wait & kitchen staff only. In a banquet room, it is also for the guests: usually with no hostess bringing the guests to the table, the guests are told which table they are assigned.

At each sitting, on the show plate or elsewhere, a small folded card indicates the name of each guest.

DRESSING THE TABLES

Once the tables are positioned and covered with felting, they are to be dressed.

When long tables are to be set, it is unlikely that a single tablecloth can be used. Each tablecloth must be of the same width, and each one overlaps the other for a few inches. Tablemats then top the tablecloths.

When large round tables are used, round tablecloths and tablemats are used, instead of the square or rectangular ones.

POSITIONING THE CHAIRS

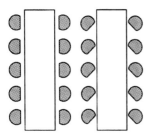

When long tables are used, it is imperative that they are perfectly aligned, just like all other tools and equipment on the table.

A final perfect touch is to place them at a 45^0 angle, as if the table is opening.

SEATING SET-UP

In a banquet situation, the entire menu and wines are known and will be served to every guest with minor changes for some individuals. Therefore all plates, silverware and glasses must be on the table. This will facilitate and expedite service.

PLATES

Show plates are rarely used. as the menu, *and sometimes napkin*, is in the center of each seat.

The only plates on the table are the bread plates.

SILVERWARE

All silverware must be positioned around where the entrée plate will be. They are placed sequentially, the first silverware used on the outside, the last in the inside.

They must be placed at 45^0 angle, with the inside silverware closed to the rim of the table.

The cheese knife & fork and dessert fork & spoon are placed above where the entrée plate will be and parallel to the table; the cheese knife at the bottom, the cheese fork, followed by the dessert spoon then the dessert fork. The silverware handles are placed each on the opposite side, according to which hand will be used: cheese knife and dessert spoon on the right, cheese and dessert forks on the left.

GLASSES

All glasses are also set on the table, the first wine glass that will be served on the left, continuing across until the last red wine glass.

The water glass is placed on the left, the champagne flute above it. Positioned in a straight line (at a 45^0 angle) this line rejoins the opposite line of glass whenever possible.

MISCELLANEOUS

Salt / Pepper Shakers

They are set in a group, one set easily accessible to a group of four guests.

Flowers

On long banquet tables, flower arrangements form a long line in the middle of the table. On large round tables, a single bouquet is placed in the center.

CONCLUSION

The most important thing is to set silverware, glasses, all tools and the table and chairs in absolute symmetry.

In some cases, strings are used to achieve this goal: one person holds the string at one end of the table while another one holds it at the other end *(an old fashioned way that still works!).*

The Art of Hosting

CHAPTER 4

Buffet Set-up

Buffets are more and more popular these days (e.g. Sunday brunch), and are used for many occasions instead of banquets. It allows individuals (instead of a banquet group), to benefit from a lower cost of dining entertainment than what is usually a fine dining establishment that most may not be able to afford.

At the same time it gives them access to a large variety of fine foods with unlimited access ("all-you-can-eat"), all for a fixed price. Therefore, a buffet is a completely different set-up: in restaurant's dining rooms and banquets, the food is served in sequence by the wait staff, necessitating a high labor cost.

On the contrary, in a buffet, most of the food is prepared and displayed on large dishes (bowls, mirrors, chaffing dishes, etc.) before the guests arrive around the dining room. This is a time where the kitchen staff comes in the dining room to work at cook's stations (carving, pastas, desserts, etc.) and serve guests' plates directly from them, thus partially eliminating the wait staff's need. The choice of food is in a sense limited, as guests cannot order anything other than what is offered on the buffet tables.

The dressed tables have a very limited set-up. Wait staff number is also limited, as the guests themselves primarily do the service. Wait stations are wider and staff duties are easier, as they are limited to serving drinks and clearing dirty dishes while guests go back to the buffet.

A buffet's success depends mainly on the presentation of a large display of a variety of foods, in addition to impeccable service. During the whole time, wait staff must be concentrated on:

1. supplying guests with a constant supply of beverages, cocktails and wines,

2. clearing the table after each plate has been emptied,

3. crumbing and cleaning the tablecloth as much as possible and,

4. helping restock food displays when low on the buffet.

POSITIONING TABLES

As the buffet is the primarily focus of the whole dining room, tables and chairs are placed away from the buffet tables (sometimes placed all around the room). At nighttime or for special occasions, a dance floor is set in the middle (or the opposite corner of the buffet). Besides this rule, the tables, table numbering and chair positions remain basically the same as in a normal dining room setting.

GUEST TABLE SET-UP

The most casual way of dining does not require a sophisticated table set-up. Tables must have salt and pepper shakers, flower vase, napkins and water glasses, silverware (large fork and knife), no other plates than the bread plate (all other plates are taken by guests when they fill up their plate at the buffet tables), or glasses other than the water glass (the wait staff should take specific drink orders for each table/guest).

SERVERS' STATIONS

For buffets, servers' stations use are limited to storage of sodas, water and beverage supply, folded napkins (or roll-ups), tablecloths, condiments and guest check preparation.

For convenience, bus pans (a plastic tub for carrying dirty dishes to the kitchen) should be placed on a rolling cart covered with a small tablecloth. It should have three bus pans per cart, separating silverware, plates and glasses in one bus pan.

No wait/tableside cart or after-dinner drink carts are to be used at a buffet.

BUFFET TABLE SETTING

It is the wait staff's duty to prepare the buffet tables where food will be displayed and chef's stations will be used. The most common and practical tables used are folding tables. They must be placed one against each other in a straight line. Some half-moon (or wavy) tops are sometimes placed on the table in intervals to break the monotony of a series of long tables.

DRESSING THE TABLE

As the buffet table is always away from any other guest's tables, it is widely visible. Therefore, it must be dressed impeccably. There are two ways to dress the table according to whether pre-made skirts are available or not:

- WITH PRE-MADE SKIRTS

1. TABLECLOTH:

Tablecloths used for buffets are wide enough to cover only the tabletop and hang all around the table by about 6 inches. Place them seam inside next to each other, one overlapping the other slightly, from one end of the table to the other.

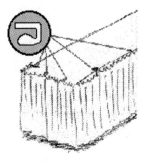

2. SKIRTS:

Nowadays, specially made, slightly folded long pieces of material that clip on the tabletop to about 2 inches from the floor exist. Attach the clips to the table rim on the side facing the guests.

- WITHOUT PRE-MADE SKIRTS

When the buffet is an occasional affair, tablecloth skirts are often not available. You must know how to dress the buffet properly without them. Tablecloths will cover the top of the table while forming a skirt all around the guests' visible side.

POSITIONING TABLECLOTH

Tablecloths must be wide enough to cover the top of the table with a hanging part of about 6 inches on the cook's side, and on guests' side, they must all be of the exact same length, the bottom being at about 2 inches from the floor.

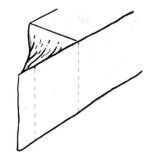

Start at one end of the table by positioning the first tablecloth as above. In addition, on the guests' side, extend the length of the tablecloth to the length of the return side, plus 6 inches.

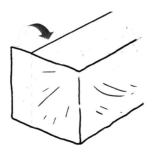

On the long side, fold the tablecloth over the width of the table by starting exactly at the guests' angle of the table rim to the opposite, then 6-in. on the cook side. Secure the folds by using pins from the inside of the tablecloth, the pin ends towards the table rim.

Once the table is completely wrapped, place a second smaller tablecloth that covers the entire tabletop with an additional 6-inch drop all around. As a substitute, use a series of smaller wide tablecloths. Place them in a diamond pattern with about 6-inches hanging down from the top of the table.

CHEF & COOKS' STATIONS

Some of the food displayed on a buffet requires chef or cook's assistance, so a number of chef/cook stations are spread along the buffet tables. These stations might include:

- Omelet station
- Waffle/pancake station
- Raw shellfish station
- Carving station
- Pasta station
- Dessert station

If these stations require electricity for equipment and/or heating lamps, but are not next to electrical outlets, extension cords must be run to stations (*underneath* the tables, in order to avoid accidents). It is always wise to use duct tape over any exposed wires.

Some cook's equipment requires high amperage, such as heavy-duty electric waffle makers. This needs to be tested prior to the first time a buffet is set-up in a dining room.

CHAFING DISHES

A location needs to be prepared before hot food can be brought to the buffet. In order to stay hot, the food is displayed in "chafing dishes". A chafing dish is no more than a fancy-looking "double-boiler". Their shapes vary from round and tall (for soups), to round and shallow (for sauces), to square or rectangular (for meat, seafood and vegetables).

A chafing dish has five components:

THE SUPPORT

It has generally four legs for stability.

At its bottom it has openings where the heating elements are placed later over a saucer.

THE HEATING ELEMENTS

They can be electric, or most commonly, small cans filled with solid or liquid fuel (commonly called burners, or "Sternos").

A saucer is placed at the center of the support's bottom circle (to avoid spilling and igniting the tablecloth).

Then the burner can is placed on the saucer. The burner's lifetime is approximately 4-6 hours; this time is usually enough for the duration of the buffet. After every buffet, discard the burners, as they will be useless. Burners are lit just before the food is brought to the buffet.

THE WATER INSERT

This consists of a large container that is inserted inside the support. Just before the food is to be brought to the buffet table, the water inserts are filled with 2-3 inches of boiling water.

THE COVER (LID)

There are two kinds: the lid, which has to be removed in order to have access to the food, or the roll top that opens from 90^0 to a full 180^0 position for serving versatility.

THE FOOD INSERT

The food insert, often called the "hotel pan", has the same shape as the water insert, but is shallower. This is the top of the "Bain-Marie" or double boiler. These inserts are filled by the cooks in the kitchen and brought to the chafing dishes by the wait-staff just before the guests' arrival.

ICEBOATS

Dishes that are served cold must be placed either on top of expensive refrigerated equipment or, most of the time, into "iceboats", i.e. containers full of ice.

Place the empty, clean iceboat at its proper location with an additional tablecloth underneath (it will not be possible to remove it after being loaded without causing the tablecloths to crumple, upsetting the entire buffet table look!); once filled up with ice, the condensation will spread over the tablecloth.

Iceboats have a drain that will allow the melted ice to evacuate. Secure the pipe from the iceboat outlet down to a 5-gallon bucket, which is hidden below the buffet table.

Fill the iceboat with ice cubes or crushed ice up to 6-in. from the top (large bowls and serving dishes will be inserted later, slightly elevating the ice cube level).

When using a carved ice sculpture, the iceboat must be absolutely level. Inside the iceboat, place a folded tablecloth, the same width as the iceboat, but double the length. This will prevent the sculpture from sliding. The tablecloth must be perfectly flat to be able to accommodate the flat bottom of the ice carving. Once the sculpture is secured, surround it with crushed ice.

Occasionally a waterproof lamp is installed to light up the carving. This will require an electric extension cord that must be placed away from any water source (*see page 48 "CHEF and COOK'S STATIONS" for additional information*).

DECORATING THE BUFFET

Now that the buffet tables are set, it is time to prepare them to receive bread platters and baskets, foods platters, food dishes, salad bowls, mirrors, chaffing dishes, ice-carvings, plates and silverware.

BOXES

The buffet tables are flat, so they need to be attractively arranged, forming different levels that also display foods securely. Square or rectangular boxes are used (already made mirror boxes or others, or any sturdy plastic, cardboard or stainless steel boxes, wrapped in small tablecloth. First cover the top and put the end of the tablecloth inside the opening of the box.). They must be of varying heights.

CENTERPIECES

They are placed at intervals and in each station, and especially where the food display is "flat", e.g. mirrors, desserts, etc. They include ice craving & pastillage sculptures made by the Chef, bouquets of flowers and branches of palm tree or other foliage spread in between food displays.

During the service, food displays must be refilled; all these decorative elements must be placed away from the future traffic to keep the refill process easy and smooth.

OTHER DECORATIONS

They include equipment that must be placed harmoniously with the other centerpieces, and usually away from the food (*see page 54*).

MIRRORS

Chefs very often display cold food—including appetizers, fish and seafood, cold cuts, cheeses and pastries—on mirrors.

They are kept in the kitchen's walk-in cooler until ready to be brought to the dining room. As with all cold food, they must be placed away from any hot food (chafing dishes).

Plan plenty of room on the buffet tables when setting up the buffet decoration.

Place the mirrors at angles to break monotony, elevating the guests' opposite side slightly to give the mirror more visual appeal.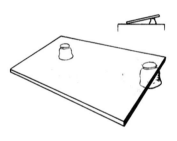

The elevation is made by secure and study pieces such as upside-down soup cups, small blocks of wood, etc.

Place the different mirrors in staggered rows to avoid monotony, as shown below.

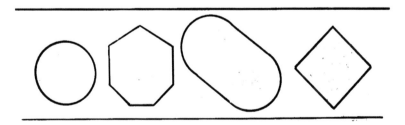

Place sufficient and adequate serving silverware on small plates around these mirrors for the guests' self-serving.

OTHER EQUIPMENT

To compensate for the limited wait staff service that a buffet has, some other equipment is needed on the buffet tables. Instead of being served, the guests go the buffet to help themselves.

Following are some examples of this equipment:

- ❖ Coffee, decaf, ice tea silver urns
- ❖ Cold flat beverage fountains
- ❖ Electric soup kettles
- ❖ Sneeze guards

This equipment is usually grouped by category in one part of the dining room.

CHAPTER 5

Taking Guests' Orders

Taking the guest's order is a crucial part of the dining experience. Since the guest's meal depends on his or her order, this is a time when your professionalism is of the utmost importance. The order must be taken in its entirety, without omission and with perfect precision. Coming back to the guest's table afterwards to ask for clarification is both embarrassing and unprofessional.

Since the guests have either made their choices or not, ordering is no longer the time for you to make suggestions or recommendations—the suggestions and recommendations are now absolutes!

Introduction

Selling the Order

Guest Positions

Writing the Check

Cocktail Orders

Food Order

Wine Order & Marrying Wine with Food

INTRODUCTION

This is also the first time you are going to the table, so welcome the guests and introduce yourself—and smile! Your smile is free of charge, represents your personality and demonstrates your willingness to serve at the best of your ability. The smile is of such importance that it is an integral part of the whole event: the décor, ambiance, food, wines, desserts, coffee and the service you give to the guests.

Also, keep in mind that while you're at the table, you must forget all your problems; your guests came to have a good time, relax and enjoy, not listen to your problems or get an attitude. Just as with a movie, if it is mediocre, chances are it will not be remembered; if it is very good or very bad, chances are it will always be remembered!

Guests know they are going to spend money, but they want their money's worth. A pleasant, smiling server has a greater chance of receiving a better reward when the check is paid. Go to the table regularly: if not, guests feel abandoned.

BEFORE THE SHIFT

Before each shift, the Chef will read the specials to the entire wait staff. This is to ensure that all wait staff knows the daily specials, and can answer any questions when asked by the guests. Make sure you understand each dish and do not be afraid to ask questions of the Chef; after all, he is here for that purpose. You will not have this opportunity after!

The following is usually covered at all menu readings:
- All featured items
- Special cooking instructions and methods of preparation
- How dishes will be served, garnished, merchandised, etc.
- Logistical problems between kitchen and dining room.
- Items that are 86'd (unavailable or have run out)

SELLING THE ORDER

The following sequence describes how to approach guests with a touch of class. The guests have just being seated; it is now time to go the table and introduce yourself. Here's a good example to use upon your fist approach to every table:

> "Good afternoon/evening (Sir/Madam). My name is _____ and I will be serving you this afternoon/evening."

If guests already have menus, and before taking a beverage or drink order, also say:

> "If you have a moment, I would like to describe the features the Chef has recommended today."

Be prepared to give a brief description of each, as explained by the Chef earlier; it is an informative and pleasurable narration for your guests. A commonly asked question in every restaurant is:

> "What's good this evening?"

If you answer: "Everything is good", you lose the opportunity to sell. You will just be an order taker. Instead, follow up with what is sensational and then *sell* the baked foie gras in puff pastry topped with a black truffle demi-glaze … Get the point?

The following are examples of the perfect description of specials, along with important points to remember:

- Talk loud and slow enough for every guest at the table to hear and understand
- Do not mumble like you are embarrassed
- Do not talk too long: be specific and concise
- When describing the dishes and their components, get excited, but don't overdo it
- Never give prices, unless asked

Suppose you ask one of your friends "How was the movie last night". If he replies: "it's good", would you go and see it? If he says: "It's great! The special effects are unbelievable! The first ten minutes will blow you away!" would you go? You probably would. Why? Your friend had excitement in his voice and used his personality to persuade you. It is powerful to describe a few words to "wet your appetite". *He was actually SELLING you this movie!*

Now its time to take the beverage/drink order:

> "I'll let you make your choice and in the meantime, may I get you a glass of wine or a cocktail?"

Send the order, pick it up and bring it to the table immediately. Serve the order and then say:

> "Are you ready to order?"

If guests immediately order an entrée, try to sell an appetizer or soup before (especially if you know that the entrée will take a while to be prepared), and say:

> "Would you like a cup of our home-made 'X' soup or a light appetizer while your entrée is being prepared?"

Send your order without delay. Go back and take the wine order:

> "Have you made your wine selection?"

If the guest is undecided, offer to suggest a choice of wines that will marry the guests' choice. Pick up the wine at once (if you wait, you may lose a second bottle...) Make sure that the proper glasses are on the table before bringing the wine (*see serving wines by the bottle, Chapter 7*)

After guests have started and tasted the first course, go back to the table and ask:

> "Is everything prepared to your satisfaction?"

You are NOT looking for trouble, but just inquire immediately so you can rectify any mistake(s) before it is too late. Repeat the request after each course. A variation could be:

"Is everything to your taste?"

When dessert time comes, guests are usually full. Again remember you are a salesperson. Then best is to bring the dessert cart or silver tray (if available) along with the dessert and the after drink menu(s). If not, try this:

"I would like to present/describe our fresh baked desserts to you. Here we have a fresh fruit tart baked in a mini piecrust with vanilla filling, etc... (describe all desserts), and last but not least, for those on a special diet we offer fresh strawberries and pineapple dipped in white and dark chocolate or plain with or without Chantilly cream. Now which one would you like?"

You will be amazed of the results you will receive! Now it's time for hot beverages.

"Would you care for coffee or hot tea, or may I suggest our Italian espresso, or our outstanding foamy cappuccino? How about treating yourself to a cordial or our imported Cognacs and fruit brandies?"

This example is excellent suggestive selling, as the purpose of selling is to sell more items, thereby increasing the guests' check, meaning your tips. Make sense?

Carefully look at the following page to see how you can earn more!

HOW TO EARN MORE

Here is a simple example:

Sell	1 more bottle of wine per shift	$15.00
Sell	6 extra glasses of wine per shift @$4.00	$24.00
Trade-Up	6 drinks from well to premium brands (.50)	$3.00
Sell	2 extra appetizers per shift (average $5.00)	$10.00
Sell	2 extra salads per shift ($3.50)	$7.00
Sell	2 extra desserts per shift ($4.00)	$8.00

Total extra sales per shift		$67.00
Extra tips earned in that shift	($67.00 x 15%)	$10.05
Extra tips every week	($10.05 x 5 days)	$50.25
Extra tips for a full year		$2,613.00

Fill out this simple worksheet to figure how much more you are going to take home just by selling a few more beverages and food items per shift at the restaurant you are working at now!

SELL	AVERAGE PRICE	TOTAL
___ extra bottles of wine	_____	_____
___ extra wines by the glass	_____	_____
___ extra pitchers of beer	_____	_____
___ drinks tradeups to premium	_____	_____
___ beer tradeups	_____	_____
___ extra appetizers	_____	_____
___ appetizers tradeups	_____	_____
___ extra salads	_____	_____
___ salads tradeups	_____	_____
___ entrées tradeups	_____	_____
___ extra desserts	_____	_____
___ extra after dinner drinks	_____	_____
___ coffee tradeups	_____	_____

The Art of Hosting

For "GUESTS POSITION": refer to Chapter 1, page 15

WRITING THE ORDER

Even though many of today's restaurants use a computer system to send orders to the kitchen, the old fashioned method of writing orders by hand is still very much alive. Although computer systems are very handy—they're excellent for management, since all types of information and reports can be pulled out—power failures happen, so you'll be glad that you wrote the order properly and legibly.

Here are the proper steps for taking a guest's order:
- Write the table number and number in the party (Top)
- Take the cocktail order for each guest, starting at position #1 and continuing around the table clockwise.
- Circle each lady's position number.
- Always take the orders in the following sequence:
    1. Oldest lady to the youngest lady
    2. Oldest gentleman to the youngest

Repeat these steps for the food order, then later for the desserts, hot beverages and finally for the after dinner drinks.

```
TABLE#: 24    PARTY#: 2

 (1)     Margarita- N/S
  2    -W - OTR side soda

 (1)     lobster Bisque
  2      Dz. escargots

 (1)    Dover almandine
       w/rice + sautéed  spin
  2    Au Poivre  MBOS

 ½ Macon Blanc    Jv
  1    Beauj. Villages  BG
```

COCKTAIL ORDER

Cocktails are the first order that is taken. The guests just sat at the table and are ready to start their dining experience. They are hungry and thirsty, so take the order quickly.

Guests usually know what cocktail they are going to have. Stand in one position and, making eye contact, take the order. Just like all the service you are going to give, the drink order is taken beginning from the oldest lady to the youngest, the oldest man to the youngest, indicating in front of each order the position number.
Once the order is taken with accuracy, send it immediately to the service bar.

COCKTAIL ORDER ABBREVIATIONS

When sending your cocktail order to the service bar, you must be specific, so the bartender can process your order fast. Indicate the level and type of liquor that you request by marking:

1. The brand to be used. Be specific, since many brands of liquor have different levels of quality, age and price. If the customer does not specify a brand, you may ask if they have a specific brand preference (which, incidentally, is an excellent way to increase your total ticket amount, since call and top-shelf brands cost more than well brands). If they do not have a preference, the bartender will pour the house's 'well' brand, which is the least expensive.

W	WELL
C	CALL
P	PREMIUM
SP	SUPER PREMIUM
TS	TOP SHELF

2. The abbreviation detailing your drinks:

D	DASH
UP	STRAIGHT UP
N	NEAT
OTR or	
/R or **R**	ON THE ROCKS
SPL	SPLASH
N/S	NO SALT
W/S	WITH SALT

If a customer asks for a splash in their drink, you must ask, "a splash of what?" Drinks can be made with a splash of water (the most common), a splash of soda, tonic or other mixer. To get the correct drink from the bartender, you must be specific.

Many, if not most, drinks can be made straight up or on the rocks (e.g., Martinis and Manhattans), so be sure to ask if the customer does not specify, and indicate their preference on the check. Other drinks, like a Cosmopolitan, are always served straight up. (*see Chapter 6, page 83*)

FOOD ORDER

All wait staff must have intensive and thorough training in the kitchen, so they know how the dishes are made and presented. They must also know which silverware and underliner to use, and be able to locate all equipment needed to accompany and serve the dishes.

When the Chef makes weekly or daily specials, a general wait staff meeting occurs prior to the opening of the restaurant. All dishes are explained: how they are prepared, presented, served, garnished, merchandized, what can be altered or not, and how to order them in the kitchen. Learn about items that are out of stock (called '86 items', which are usually written on a chalk board in the kitchen), and be ready to advise the guests prior to taking any food order. Don't be afraid to take notes during this meeting, as it may help later to review and memorize them.

Your presence at such meetings is absolutely mandatory, since it avoids the embarrassment of saying, "I don't know...let me ask the Chef" when you're taking the guests' order.

The cocktails have just been served, and now it is time to disrupt the guests with the food order so the first thing is to apologize for any interruption and ask if the guests are ready to order. And remember, keep smiling!

A note when taking orders: your preferences and personal taste are absolutely irrelevant and should not be mentioned in any way. Do not make comments like, "Good choice", "That's one of my favorites" etc. Be ready to answer any questions with clarity and knowledge.

SPECIAL OF THE DAY

First, describe each special, mentioning only its major components—guests do not need to know the exact recipe. Besides, you can always go into greater detail upon the guest's request. Speak slowly and clearly so you can be understood and heard by everyone.

FISH

This chart identifies different species of fish that share similar characteristics of flavor and texture. You will be able to advise the guests while becoming familiar with the wide variety of fish.

FLAVOR

		MILD	MODERATE	FULL
TEXTURE	DELICATE	Alaska pollok Flounder Orange Roughy Sea trout Skate Sole Weakfish	Catfish Hake Pink Salmon Whiting	Butterfish Eel Herring Sardine Smelt
	MEDIUM FIRM	Breams Cod Cusk Grouper Haddock Halibut Ocean Pout Skate Snapper Tilapia Titlefish Wolffish	Atlantic Pollock Black Sea Bass Buffalofish Chum Salmon Drums Mahi-Mahi Ocean Perch Perch Pompano Porgy-scup Rainbow Trout Striped Bass	Amberjack Atlantic Salmon Bluefish Carp King Salmon Mackerel Pomfret Sablefish Sockeye Salmon Yellowtail
	FIRM	Kingklip Monkfish	Shark Sturgeon	Chilean Seabass Swordfish Tuna

MEAT DONENESS

When taking most red meat or fish orders (including tuna, veal and game meat), the doneness must be asked for and indicated on the order:

Abbreviation	Doneness	Description
B/B	Black & Blue:	The meat is charred on the outside, while the inside remains raw.
B	Blue:	The meat is sizzled enough just to eliminate the outside raw color.
R	Rare:	The meat is sizzled on the grill on the outside, while the inside remains raw.
MR	Medium-Rare:	The meat is still red in color, but the center is warm.
M	Medium:	Only a very small fraction of the center is still reddish.
MW	Medium-Well:	The meat is cooked until it is red, but there is no more blood showing
W	Well-Done:	The meat is cooked thoroughly and is no longer soft to the touch.

EXCEPTION TO THE RULE

Never ask for the doneness of the "end-cut" of a roasted Prime-Rib: IT IS ALWAYS WELL-DONE!

Sometimes guests complain that their meat is not cooked as requested. The proper way to verify the doneness of the meat is by cutting it in the center.

GARNISH CHANGES

When vegetables and starches are specifically mentioned in the menu description of the dish and the guest wants to switch one vegetable (or starch) or another one, be precise and clearly indicate the change by underlining it. If the establishment charges for such changes, don't forget to do it.

SIDE ORDERS

Some guests may require either a side order of extra vegetable (or starch) or that they be dished on a separate plate so the entrée be free of either vegetables or starch.

SOS

When the sauce of a dish is requested to be on the side, specify this on your order by indicating "SOS" (*for* **S***auce* **O***n the* **S**ide) next to it.

The Art of Hosting

WINE ORDER

Wines are a substantial part of the guest's check (and of your tip), so always present the wine list with the menu when seating your guests. Wines must complement the food being served. Only after the cocktail and food orders have been taken, can you then take the wine order and make recommendations (upon the guest's request). A professional Captain or Waiter never leaves the guest without having a wine order. Any other drinks or beverages, including water, are a disgrace to any meal and the one who prepared it!

MARRYING WINE WITH FOOD

Marrying wine with food is a very subjective topic, as there are NO 100% correct answers! Many lengthy books cover every possible rule of conduct in the wine world; however, marrying wine with food is a matter of taste. Therefore, *the host must follow the guest's taste*.

If the guest requests your advice, here are some general guidelines to follow:

- Suggest a wine from the same origin as the dish
- Champagne, from the beginning of the meal, complements dishes until red meat is served
- White wine with seafood, and red wine with meat is a rule that can be broken: a dry rosé or a light red is perfectly acceptable with fish (e.g. a thick, oily fish such as tuna or salmon complements a medium red wine, like a Pinot Noir)
- Observe the unconditional golden rule: "red wine with dark meat; white, rosé, light red with light meat". The lighter the meat, the lighter the wine, stronger the meat, the stronger the wine
- Always serve the same wine the dish/sauce was cooked with

68

- If a large array of flavors and types of dishes was ordered by the guests at the table, suggest a light red or a dry rosé
- With sweet dishes suggest a slightly less-sweet wine, but with a similar level of sweetness as the food itself
- High acid foods (e.g. tomato, citrus dishes) go well with Sauvignon Blanc
- With rich, fatty foods (duck, goose, lamb) go a Loire Rouge, red Chianti, oaky Chardonnay, Gamay or Gewürztraminer
- Spicy, smoked dishes balance well with a fruitier light wine such as Gamay, Sauvignon Blanc, or Gewürztraminer
- A hearty stew *(cooked without wine)* goes well with a rich and hearty wine such as a Petite Syrah

Do not serve more that three wines in the course of one meal (including Champagne). In a restaurant where guests usually do not eat the same dishes, offer a light wine that will blend with all dishes. Below are the general guidelines for each dish

- German wines are perfect with smoked, cured or spicy dishes
- Chardonnay's buttery aroma matches with butter sauces, cream pasta, lobster and other shellfish
- Sauvignon Blanc, with its crispness, is perfect with oysters, herb flavored vegetables, tomatoes and citrus dishes
- Chilled rosé is the only wine that can accompany curry dishes

WINE DON'Ts

While there are no hard-and-fast rules for marrying wines with food, there are nevertheless absolute rules on what *not* to serve with specific dishes. Here are some of them:

- Never serve sparkling water with food
- Never serve more than three wines in the course of the meal
- Never serve sweet wine with fish, or dry wine with dessert
- Never serve red Burgundy with asparagus
- Never serve *Vintage* Red with seafood or fish
- If salad is served after the main entrée (the typical and traditional French style), suggest still water, as the acidity of the dressing will kill any wine

APERITIFS

Whenever possible, avoid strong alcohol drinks as they are too aggressive to allow the palate to appreciate most first courses. The aperitif *par excellence* in every conceivable situation is Champagne, followed by a Kir or Kir-Royale.

STARTERS

ANTIPASTI	*Light* Chianti, Chenin Blanc, Gamay, *Rosé wines*
ASPARAGUS	Champagne, Muscat d'Alsace, Chardonnay,
ARTICHOKE	Sauvignon Blanc from the Loire Valley (France), Arbois Rosé (France), Schilcher (Austria)
AVOCADO	Champagne, Chablis, Gewürztraminer, Muscadet
CAVIAR	Champagne is the best; Vodka is definitely **not** acceptable!

EGGS	Any type *(including Omelets, Quiches, and savory Souffles)* Champagne, Sparkling Whites
ESCARGOTS	Macon Blanc, Beaujolais, *light* Chianti, Gamay
FOIE GRAS	Champagne demi-sec, Graves, Sauternes, Traminer, Gewürztraminer, Tokay d'Alsace
GARLIC BUTTER	Serve the wine recommended for the main ingredient
MEAT PLATTER	Beaujolais, Gamay, Valpolicella, *light* Chianti
MOUSSES	Serve the wine recommended for the Main ingredient *(meat, fowl, fish or vegetable)*
PÂTÉS	*Same as above*
PASTA	*As an appetizer:* Sparkling White, Chardonnay
PROSCIUTTO	Riesling, *light* Chianti
RICE/RISOTTO	*As an appetizer:* Sparkling White, Chardonnay
SALADS *As an appetizer with vinaigrette dressing:*	Alsace, Manzanilla, Sherry, Fino, Gewürztraminer
As an appetizer with other dressings:	Sauvignon Blanc
As an appetizer with warm ingredients:	Champagne
After main entrée (French style):	Water
SEAFOOD PLATTER (including oysters and clams on-the-half-shell, cooked/cold shrimp and lobster, etc):*	Muscadet, Champagne nature, Gros-Plant, Pinot Grigio, Riesling
SMOKED FISH	Sauvignon Blanc

SOUPS	*Purée, Velouté, Cream & chilled Soup:*	Champagne
	Lobster/Shrimp Bisque:	Champagne Rosé
	Game soups:	Côtes-du-rhône, Rioja, Bordeaux, Burgundy
	Minestrone/tomato soup:	Lambrusco, Sauvignon Blanc

FISH & SEAFOOD

Seafood is traditionally served with dry white wines and sparkling wines, but rosé and red are possible in certain circumstances.

FISH *with sauce:*	*Serve the wine used to make the sauce*
FISH Stews:	*Serve the wine (red or white) used to cook the stew*
"Au gratin":	Sauvignon Blanc
"Deep Fried":	Pouilly-Fuissé, Pinot Grigio, Gamay, *light* Chianti
Butter sauces:	Chardonnay

BOUILLABAISSE	White or rosé : Provence, Champagne, Cassis Rosé
CIOPPINO	Chardonnay
COD	Muscadet, Pinot Blanc, Pinot Grigio, Vinho Verde, Crémant d'Alsace
CRAYFISH	Sancerre, Pouilly Fumé
DOVER SOLE	Champagne Blanc-de-Blanc, Muscadet, Pinot Blanc, Pinot Grigio, Vinho Verde
EEL	Vouvray, Sauvignon Blanc, Gamay, Beaujolais,
HADDOCK	Muscadet, Pinot Blanc, Pinot Grigio, Vinho Verde, Crémant d'Alsace
HAKE	Muscadet, Pinot Blanc, Pinot Grigio, Vinho Verde, Crémant d'Alsace

HALIBUT	Muscadet, Pinot Blanc, Pinot Grigio, Vinho Verde, Crémant d'Alsace
LOBSTERS	*Grand Cru* Chablis, Champagne
with sauce:	*Serve the wine (red or white) used to make the sauce*
MACKEREL	Sauvignon Blanc
PIKE	Sancerre, white Graves, Champagne
RIVERFISH	any dry Rosé wines
SALMON	Champagne (white or rosé), Sancerre, Montrachet, Chardonnay, white Burgundy, Riesling
SARDINES	Vinho Verde
SCALLOPS	*Grand Cru* Chablis, Champagne
SEA BREAM	Muscadet, Pinot Blanc, Pinot Grigio, Vinho Verde, Crémant d'Alsace
SHRIMP	Loire Sauvignon, Mosel, Sauvignon Blanc
SHELLFISH	*Grand Cru* Chablis, Champagne, Muscadet, Bourgogne Aligoté, Sauvignon Blanc
TURBOT	*Blanc-de-blanc* Champagne, Muscadet, Pinot Blanc, Pinot Grigio, Vinho Verde
TROUT	
Fresh:	Sancerre (white or rosé), Montrachet, Tavel, Pink Cava Brut, Provence
Smoked:	Gewürztraminer, Sémillon, Gamay, Beaujolais, Valpolicella

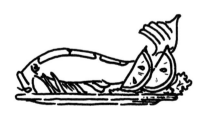

MEAT & POULTRY

Observe the unconditional golden rule:

"RED WINE WITH DARK MEAT, WHITE, ROSE, *Light* RED WINE WITH LIGHT MEAT"

The stronger the meat, the stronger the wine – the lighter the meat, the lighter the wine, and everything in between follows the golden rule.

BEEF STEAKS:	
Grilled:	Gamay, Sémillon, Beaujolais, Valpolicella
Sautéed:	Any medium, medium-full, or full body red wine
STEAK AU POIVRE	Bourgueil, Cabernet
STEWS:	
Dark stews:	Bordeaux, Burgundy, Rhône, Rioja, *The super barrique of* Tuscany
Light stews:	WHITE: Macon, French Colombard, Chenin Blanc
	RED: Beaujolais, Gamay, Bourgueil, Chinon, Pinot Noir, *light* Chianti
BISON	*Same as BEEF*
BURGERS	Côtes-du-Rhône, Cabernet Sauvignon
CURRIES	Chilled Rose, ice-cool beer or water
DUCK	Gamay (Morgon, Fleurie, Moulin-à-vent), Semillon, Valpollicella, Quinta da Bacalhôa
GAME: "Mid-hung":	Gamay, Rioja, Tokay d'Alsace, Australian Shiraz
"Full-hung":	*Full-bodied* Bordeaux *or* Burgundy, Côte Rôti, Châteauneuf-du-Pape
GOOSE	*Red* Loire *Valley,* Chianti, Riesling, Champagne, *South Africa* Chenin Blanc

KIDNEYS	Châteauneuf-du-Pape, Rioja, Médoc, Cabernet Sauvignon
LAMB	Bourgogne Rouge, light Burgundy, Gamay
LIVER:	
Calf:	Côtes-du-Rhône, Syrah
Chicken:	Gigondas, Gamay, Red Zinfandel
MEAT PIES:	
Cold:	Light red wine with white meat pies, Chinon, Bourgueil with game pies
Hot:	See *STEWS, above*
PHEASANT	Pomerol, *full-bodied* Bordeaux *or* Burgundy *(if "well-hung")*
PORK	Beaujolais, Gamay, light Chianti
POULTRY	Champagne, Alsace, Mosel, Gamay, light to medium-light red
SWEETBREAD:	
Breaded	Pouilly-Fuissé, Pinot Grigio, Gamay, *light* Chianti
Grilled	Côtes-du-Rhône, *any good* Cabernet Sauvignon
In brown sauce	Red, dry to medium-dry white, Crémant, Champagne
In cream sauce:	St-Emilion, Merlot
VEAL	*Same as PORK & POULTRY, above*

SPECIALTIES	

Boeuf Bourguignon	*Same wine it was cooked with*
CHEESE FONDUE:	
Dry white wine:	Fendant, Apremont, Crépy, Champagne
Dry red wines:	Gamay, Beaujolais
CHEESE SOUFFLE	Champagne
CHILI con carne	Chilled Rosé, ice-cool beer or ... water
COQ AU VIN	*Same wine it was cooked with*
DUCK à l'Orange	Châteauneuf-du-Pape
STROGANOFF	Cabernet Sauvignon, Merlot, medium-full body red wine,

CHEESES	

Although good red wines complement cheeses, the rule can sometimes be broken:

Blue-veined	Port, Sauternes, Tokay Gewürztraminer
BRIE	Côtes-du-rhône, Macon Rouge, Champagne, Crémant
CAMEMBERT	Beaujolais, Côtes-du-rhône
CHEDDAR	Châteauneuf-du-Pape
EDAM	Port, Sauternes, *sweet dessert wines*
EMMENTAL	Sauvignon Blanc
Goat cheeses	Beaujolais, Sancerre, Gewürztraminer
GORGONZOLA	Chianti, Tokay, red Burgundy
GOUDA	Port, Sauternes
GRUYERE	Gewürztraminer, Tokay

MOZZARELLA	Chianti
MUNSTER	Gewürztraminer, red Burgundy, Côtes-du-Rhône
PARMESAN	Chianti Classico
PROVOLONE	Red Burgundy, Pinot Grigio
ROQUEFORT	Tokay, red Burgundy, dry Sherry
Soft, mild	Beaujolais Nouveau, Champagne, Pinot Grigio
Swiss Cheese	Fendant, Apremont

DESSERTS

Apple pie	Tokay, Gewürztraminer
Apfel (Apple) Strüdel	Tokay, Gewürztraminer
Cakes	Tokay, Vouvray Pétillant, Asti Spumante, Sauternes, Champagne
Ice cream	Muscat, Champagne
Fruits	Riesling, Muscat, Asti Spumante, Vouvray Pétillant

The Art of Hosting

CHAPTER 6

Serving Drinks by-the-Glass

Glasses

Cocktails

Wines

Beers

Other Cold Beverages

Water

Hot Drinks

After-dinner Drinks

Most of these drinks are served from the service bar. They should never be carried to the table with your hands: trays have been created for this purpose—use them!

- Place a clean white napkin in the center of the tray

- Place glasses leg (stem) down in the center of the tray

- Carry the tray with your left hand underneath it. Your brain will keep it leveled

- **Never** drop the tray to the guest's table

Service them as follows:

- Using your right hand, hold each glass by its stem (never by its body: this is where the guest will put his/her lips!), place the wine glass above the knife (right) and water/beverages on top of the fork (left)
- When the table is undressed *(with no tablecloth)*, place the drink on a cocktail napkin
- When the table is dressed, the drink must go:

Rocks glass: On a small underliner (saucer) topped with a cocktail napkin. This is to avoid condensation—the chilled ice drink **will** wet the tablecloth and leave a mark for the entire meal.

Stem glass: Directly on the tablecloth, as with any wine glass.

COCKTAILS

GLASSES

Glasses are *always* stocked at the bar, where the bartender uses them in making the ordered drinks. In some restaurants, the captain, waiter or cocktail waitress has to present some glasses to the bartender in order to fill the order—another important reason to know your glasses and their use.

As an apprentice will soon discover, there is a large variety of glasses out there, each of which must be chosen according to the type of drink they will hold. Spend some time learning your glasses, as it generates sales (and increases your tips).
Drinks sold "by-the-glass" are usually served at the service bar where their bottles are located. These are some examples of the basic glasses used to serve "drinks-by-the-glass":

1. TUMBLER: *Bucket, Collins, Shot, Rocks Highball*

2. FOOTED WARE: *Cappuccino, Sherry, Piña Colada, Snifter*

3. STEMWARE: *Red Wine, Martini, White Wine, Margarita*

SMALL ICE CUBE BUCKET

To refine cocktail service, bring along a small ice cube bucket (crystal or other) with a serving spoon in it to the table.

GARNISHES

Some cocktails require garnishes that the wait staff must add to the cocktail. At the service bar, a fruit tray contains these garnishes: cherries, lemon twists, lemon & lime wedges, green olives, pearl onions (and sometimes pineapple, strawberries, oranges, banana, cucumber & kiwi slices, coconut flakes, mint sprigs, etc.)

Here are some examples of their use:

CELERY STICK	Bloody Mary
CHERRY	Brandy Alexander, Chi-Chi, Colorado Bulldog, Golden Cadillac, Grasshopper, Harvey Wallbanger, Manhattan, Mocha Frost, Mudslide, Old Fashioned, Pina Colada, Pink Lady, Pink Squirrel, Rootbeer Float, Roy Rogers, Schnappsicle, Screaming Orgasm, Shirley Temple, Toasted Almond, etc.
COCKTAIL PEARL ONION	Gibson (This is simply a Martini with an with an onion instead of an olive)

GREEN OLIVE	Gin & Vodka Martinis, Bloody Mary
LEMON QUARTER	All Long Islands Teas
LEMON TWIST	All Long Islands Teas, Bellini, Blue Hawaiian, Champagne Cocktail, Cosmopolitan, Lemon Drop, Lynchburg Lemonade, Life Saver, Perfect Manhattan, Perfect Rob Roy, Purple Hooter, Sex on the Beach, some Martini, Tidy Bowl, Wine Spritzer, Watermelon, etc.
LIME WEDGE	Gin/Soda or Tonic (All drinks with tonic in them get a lime garnish), Margarita, Vodka/Soda or Tonic and some Daiquiris, Kamikaze, Woo-Woo, etc.
LIME & CHERRY	Beetlejuice, Between-the-Sheet, Blue Hawaiian, Fuzzy Navel, Hara-Carri, Hurricane, Mai-Thai, Melon Ball, Pearl Harbor, Planters Punch, Scorpion, Sloe Gin Fizz, Sicilian Kiss, Tequila Surprise, Zombie, and all "Collins" and "Sours" cocktails.
ORANGE QUARTER	Used as a flag (with a cherry on a toothpick), upon guest's request.
PINEAPPLE	Piña Colada, other wild cocktails, cocktails having multiple fruit flavors and upon guest's request.
STRAWBERRY	Berryetto, Strawberry Margarita, Daiquiri, & Colada

COCKTAILS WITH NO GARNISHES

After Five, Alabama Slammer, B-52, Baybreeze, Black/White Russian, Cape Cod, French Connection, Godfather/mother, Greyhound, Jellybean, Madras, Mimosa, Mind Eraser, Russian Quaalude, Rusty Nails, Samurai, Screwdriver, Seabreeze, Separator, Silk Panties, Slippery Nipple, Smith & Kerns, Snowshoe, Stinger.

> Cocktails must go to the table right away; NO questions asked!

83

WINES

WINE GLASSES

Each wine must be served in the appropriate glass:
- Chilled white and rosé wines are served in narrower, smaller glasses than red wines, since they are refilled more often with the chilled wine from the bottle.
- Room temperature red wines are served in wider-bodied glasses called *ballons,* which allow the wine's bouquet to expand in the glass. It is important to serve a good vintage wine in an even larger glass.
- Champagne & sparkling wines are served in a flute *(or tulip)* glass. A so called "Champagne cup" is to be avoided at all times, as the bouquet of the Champagne evaporates too quickly, the precious bubbles having a wide surface dissipate and you end-up too soon with a flat, tasteless drink!
- Port wine is served in a smaller glass, as it is richer that other red wines and usually served with appetizers or even desserts.

WINE CONTENT

Wine by the glass does not follow the ethical way of pouring wine when ordered by the bottle: it is a single serving, so the guest must receive his money worth. These drinks are poured at the service bar and are filled up to 1-inch from the glass rim. The volume of wine served in a glass directly affects its selling price. Some guests may complain that they had the same wine in another place at a less expensive price.

Learn the glass sizes that the house is using for each different type of wine: white & rose, red, port and sparkling, as they vary from one establishment to another, as do the selling prices!

It is conservative to say that serving 4 glasses per 750 ml. (25.4 oz.) bottle, or 6 oz. per serving is a common custom and appropriate.

SERVING WINE BY-THE-GLASS

Bring the glasses on a tray to the table (*not ON the table*). Place the wine glass above the knife (right side of the guest). There is no need for underliner or cocktail napkins, if the table is dressed (with tablecloth), otherwise, place it on a cocktail napkin.

Suggestion:	Offer a two-top (table with two guests) who ordered two glasses by-the-glass of the same wine to leave the whole bottle on the table, and offer to charge them only what they use. 75% of the time, they will empty it!

BEERS

Along with wine, beer is one of the oldest beverages known. It is only recently that beer is served chilled *(which kills most of the European beers!)* As a result, when serving European guests, ask if they want their beer chilled or just cold. Don't be surprised if some North American guests request for a saltshaker!
Never wash beer glasses with soap or detergent. Use a solution of baking soda or salt and very hot water; allow glasses to air dry

GLASSES

Beer can be served in three major different containers:
1. A German-type mug (stein)
2. A glass mug, usually frosted
3. A Pilsner glass
4. In its own bottle (which is certainly more unacceptable during the course of a meal!)

DRAFT BEER

Poured in a wet and chilled glass *(or mug)* it is foamy; therefore serve it at once over cocktail napkin, underliner or on the tablecloth *(see the previous pages)*
Served in a pitcher, place a waterproof FDA approved plastic bag filled with ice cubes to keep the beer cold.

Unusual order called "Panaché": ½ beer ½ lime / lemon soda

BY THE BOTTLE

- Never open a bottle at the service bar: some guests might be offended and doubt the veracity of the service.

- Bring the glass and the bottle on a tray to the table.

- Place it over the appropriate liner.

- Some beers ask for garnish, such as a Mexican beer (lime), which must be placed on the side dish.

FOOD & BEER

Beer is not recommended with food, although some Northern & Eastern Europeans will disagree.

When beer is the subject, recommend:

- Ale with red meat *(a restaurant chain made a name out of it)*

- A lager pairs well with fish dishes.

- Think of ale as red wine, and lager as white wine.

- Never serve beer with dessert, except with chocolate.

WATER

In the North America, it is a custom to serve a glass of water immediately when the guests sit at the table. This tradition may come from the time of horse travel, guests needing to clean their throat from the road dust.

Nowadays, water **should** be served only upon request, as it is not a necessity anymore. Help save our resources or use bottled water, which is usually more pure and of a better quality. It is also a good additional source of sales.

WATER GLASSES

Water glass shapes vary according to the class of the restaurant:

- A plastic glass is perfectly acceptable in a family-style restaurant: they keep the cost down, are affordable and don't break easily.
- 1 to 3 ☆s: a highball glass is recommended.
- 4 to 5 ☆s: a large white wine type glass (stem glass) is mandatory.

A lemon slice or quarter is sometimes served with water; although it is not recommended, as the acidity of the lemon very rarely matches with dishes, it must be then placed on the side or over the rim, but *never* inside the glass: let the guest decide.

SERVICE LOCATION

Water, just like soda, is usually dispensed at a fountain located in the waiter's station, inside the dining room or near the kitchen entrance. Therefore it is the waiter's or busboy's responsibility.

Fill each glass with ice cubes and fill the glass to 1-in. from the rim with water.

When using a High Ball style glass, place the glass onto an underliner to avoid condensation later on the tablecloth.

In a fine dining establishment, water, just like soda and cold beverages, is served by the bottle and follows the same rules as the service of wine.

WATER SERVICE

Bring the glasses on a tray to the table and place the glass:

❖ On an underliner *(when a high ball glass is used)*, or

❖ Directly on the tablecloth *(when using a stemmed glass)*.

> NOTE: A water glass must be placed above the fork *(left side of the guest)* as water is considered a secondary and incidental beverage compared to wine.

OTHER COLD DRINKS

Neither sweet drinks nor any drink containing lemon should be served with any decent meal, as they affect the taste buds and alter the flavors of most dishes.

Sugar (powdered or cubes) and sugar substitutes must be present on the table in their proper dispenser prior to serving these drinks.

As usual, if the table is dressed while using tumbler type glasses, use a small underliner under the glass, none when using a footed/stemware glass, or a cocktail napkin if the table is undressed.

FRUIT JUICES

Usually served at breakfast time, they can be ordered at lunchtime in place of soups (e.g. tomato juice). Serve them in small-footed ware or tumbler type glasses with a small underliner underneath them.

TIP   Don't hesitate to place a slice of fresh fruit either on the rim of the glass or on the side of the glass over the underliner.

ICED TEA/COFFEE

Iced coffees and teas come in different flavors, and can be sweetened or unsweetened. They are served either in footed ware or tumbler type glasses with a small underliner underneath them. Place an unwrapped straw on the side and lemon quarters on the underliner or on the rim of the glass (never inside).

SODAS

Follow the same rules as iced tea/coffee.

> TIP: Lemon quarters can also be offered with colas, lime with lime flavored sodas, cherry with cherry flavored sodas, virgin cocktails *(Shirley Temple, etc.)*

HOT DRINKS

Usually served at the end of the meal, hot drinks include coffees, teas and herbal teas, chocolate, espressos and creamed non-alcoholic coffees. All are served on a saucer topped with a doily, which is placed on a dessert plate. Sugar & sugar substitutes must be on the table prior to serving. Just like food (hot plate for hot food, cups must be presented to the guests HOT!

COFFEES

Regular and decaffeinated coffee machines are located in the wait station (dining room) or at the kitchen entrance. It is the wait staff's duty to make new coffee when the last cup is taken. Coffee must be made fresh no more than every 30-min. It is a good practice to have a check board on or next to the machines.

Coffee should be poured at the table from a coffee pot (and **not** brought already filled-up)

CHOCOLATE

A few decades ago, hot chocolate was prepared tableside in a bowl: whole milk was whipped over the coca powder. Foam was then created. The beverage was then poured, topped with the foam and finally dusted with some cocoa powder.

When already prepared, serve like coffee.

TEAS & HERB TEAS

In fine restaurants different teas and herb teas are presented to the guests; a small teapot containing hot water, placed on a saucer, is served from the right side of the guest, handle facing right.
In other restaurants, regular or decaffeinated teas are served from a teapot.

OTHER HOT COFFEES

They include Chocolat au lait, Caffe Latte, Cappuccino, etc.
Some require a garnish (e.g., sugar stick & biscotti for cappuccino). All are served on a saucer covered with a doily, everything placed on a dessert plate.

> RULE: All hot beverages must be served to the table together as soon as they are prepared: they are made hot; don't let them get cold.

SUGAR

Sugar and sugar substitutes must be on the table prior to serving hot beverages, including:

- Powdered sugar: in a sugar bowl or in bags (white & brown)

- Sugar cubes (white & brown)

- Sugar stick

- Sugar substitute

AFTER DINNER DRINKS

Only in upscale restaurants will you find an after-dinner drink cart. The cart is brought to the guests' table (where the appropriate glasses are stocked) at which point the captain/sommelier serves the after dinner drinks.

If they are not set on the after dinner drink cart, after dinner glasses are stocked at the bar/service bar, where the bartender will fill the order using the appropriate glass.

Unless you have an "after dinner/cordial cart" these drinks come from the service bar. Some of them require garnish (three coffee beans in Sambuca, etc.) that you must do yourself.

Each drink must be placed on a small plate covered with a dolly. Carry them on the tray with all necessary underliners on the side, in one single pile.

At the table, holding the tray with your left hand, bring one plate and the drink on top of it. From the tray, place the after dinner drink in the center of the guest *like any food plate.*

COFFEE COCKTAILS

When served in a glass (e.g., Irish Coffee, etc.), and as opposed to a coffee cup, follow the same instructions as the cocktails on the previous page and place them on a small underliner topped with a doily. Do not forget to put any required garnish(es) and whipped cream when called for.

Although they are usually made at the service bar, it is a good practice to offer to make some tableside to finish the celebration of the meal *and increase the total check.* The following are some tableside coffee cocktail recipes:

Café Royale

Place a lump of sugar on a spoon over a cup of hot black coffee. Pour a shot of dark rum through the lump, allowing it to run into the coffee. Light the sugar cube and allow it to burn out. Stir and serve.

Café Brûlot for 4

1 cinnamon stick, broken
4 cloves
1/2 orange peel
1/2 lemon peel
16 fl oz hot coffee
4 sugar cubes or teaspoons
2 fl oz Cognac
2 tablespoons Grand Marnier
Combine cinnamon, cloves, orange and lemon peels, and sugar in a saucepan over low heat. Stir in Cognac and liqueur. Light the mixture carefully with a long match. Slowly stir in the coffee. Stir until flame subsides. Serve in small cups.

Café del Diablo for 1

2 sugar cubes
1/2 shot Grand Marnier
1 strip orange peel
8 oz freshly brewed coffee
1 1/2 shots brandy
6 cloves
1 strip lemon peel
Heat all of the ingredients, except the coffee, in a saucepan. Pour the hot coffee into a mug. Use a long match to light the brandy and allow the flame to burn. The flame should subside in about 20 seconds. Pour the brandy mixture over the coffee, stir and enjoy.

Orleans Coffee for 4	Brew a very strong pot of gourmet coffee for 4 people. Stud a strip of orange peel with a couple of cloves for each and place in the bottom of 4 heatproof glasses or tall cups with a dash of grated lemon peel and a teaspoon of dark brown sugar. Pour 5 tablespoons each of Cognac and Benedictine into a small pan, heat, and then ignite. Pour the flaming liquid into the glasses. Pour the coffee on top and allow to cool slightly.

BRANDIES

There are two kinds of brandy:

- The 'white *fruit* brandies' that must be served chilled in an ice-frosted snifter, and
- The "oak aged brandies" that are served in a room temperature snifter.

Served straight, they require no garnish, but it is customary to serve sugar cubes on the side on a small plate.

CORDIALS & LIQUEURS

These are served in different glass shapes and sizes that the bartender will use.

Very few require a garnish such as three coffee beans in a straight up Sambuca that is served in a snifter.

Like brandies, they are placed on a small plate covered with a doily, and all placed on a dessert plate.

CHAPTER 7

Serving Wines by the Bottle

While food dishes must be carried on a tray, this does not apply for bottles of wines:

- A white or rosé wine is brought to the table in an ice bucket
- Old vintage red wines are brought in a basket

Other red wines are brought by hand *(a bottle carried on a tray is unstable)*

Contrary to food, wines are poured at the right side of the guest (where glasses are placed), but bottles are always presented to the guest on his or her left.

When handling the bottle for pouring the wine, confusing rules apply:

1. White wine - the label is shown (if a napkin is not used). The reasons are:
   - The bottle is in the ice bucket: nobody can see the label,
   - If held by the moist label (and its glue), chances are that the label will crumple and your hand will accidentally drop the bottle.

2. Red wine - the label is hidden because:
   - Any sediments are on the opposite side of the label and, although the bottle is moved several times to pour the wine, it is not as bad as if it was turned upside down
   - The bottle will stay on the table for every one to see the label until the bottle is empty.

After the guest who ordered the wine gives his or her approval, serve the oldest to the youngest ladies first, then the oldest to the youngest men, finally finishing with the guest who ordered the bottle.

TIP   Pour each glass to a third, making sure that you will have enough wine for all the guests.

BEFORE SERVING WINES

WINE SERVICE TIPS:

- Learn your Wine List, by the bottle and by the glass
- Know the temperature of different wines
- Be prepared to give a brief description of each
- Know how to marry wine with food and make recommendations
- Serve wines as rapidly as you can, right after you send the food order to the kitchen - you may increase your chance of a re-order

WINE STORAGE

All wines are stored in a cellar, where they can be kept for years, if it meets the following standards:
- Cool temperature with no harsh temperature variations
- Dark environment, away from any light
- No vibration

Wine bottles are stored in compartments, separating vintage and origin. Bottles are stacked **label up**: The label, along with the foil capsule, is the 'dress' of the bottle—if stacked label-down, the label will be damaged, even partially destroyed.

After months and years, sediments drop on the opposite side of the bottle.

No departure from the vintage red wines rule is permitted. Therefore wine bottles must be transported from one area to the next gently, respecting the label position, and obviously without shaking them!

When ready to be brought to the dining room, do so with a minimum of handling. They are then stored in the 'cave du jour' (cellar of the day) where their temperature will slowly raise to the room temperature. They must stay there for a minimum of 24 hours before being served.

Just like the cellar, the 'cave du jour' must be away from light and vibration.

In view of the above, when an old vintage red wine is ordered, the same care for transportation has to be respected: the bottle is placed slowly into a wine basket (label up, *of course*) and brought gently to the table.

As most old vintage red wines contain sediments, they must be decanted (using a decanter carafe), in order to separate the clear wine from the sediments *(see drawing, page 114)*

White and sparkling wines should not be stored in a refrigerator for a long period of time: the cork will dry *(especially if, by mistake, it is stored upright)*; Sparkling wines will lose their precious gas, and both white & sparkling will have a funny rancid taste.

TEMPERATURE

The temperature of wines must be adjusted naturally, i.e. slowly. Never let a red wine bottle sit next to a fire/chimney or even worse, warm a red wine by plunging the bottle in hot water!

Here are some wine temperature guidelines:

Sweet & Liquorish White Wine, Dry Sherry (Jerez):	2-5^{0}C	35-40^{0}F
Dry White & Rosé Wines, Ciders, Champagne and Sparkling:	5-10^{0}C	40-50^{0}F
Light Red Gamay, Chianti, Valpolicella:	10-12^{0}C	50-55^{0}F
Vintage Bourgogne/Burgundy, Merlot:	14-15^{0}C	57-60^{0}F
Vintage Bordeaux, Cabernet Sauvignon:	16-18^{0}C	60-65^{0}F
Madeira, Port, Sherry (Xeres or Jerez):	5^{0}C/10^{0}F	above room temperature

WINE PREPARATION

As with the dishes served during a meal, wines need preparation. All of this must be done prior to bringing the wine to the table, to avoid confusion and mishandling of the wine. Before bringing the wine bottle to the table, the following steps must be taken:

WHITE, ROSÉ & SPARKLING

These wines must be served at their proper temperature and placed in an ice bucket.

1. Have the ice bucket stand (if available) next to the guests' table
2. Have the ice bucket filled with ice, water and a pinch of rock salt mixed in. *(if ice bucket stand is not available, place the ice bucket on a plate topped with a folded white napkin to prevent the bucket from sliding, and to avoid condensation later on the plate)*
3. Place the bottle at a 45^0 angle inside the ice bucket
4. Wrap a white napkin around the bottle to maintain the chilled temperature inside the bucket.

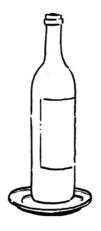

NON-VINTAGE RED WINES

They are usually young and have no sediments. When the bottle is served at the table, place it on a small flat plate on a table: this will avoid leaving a ring on the tablecloth!

WINE BASKET

VINTAGE RED WINES *that do not require decanting*:

All vintage red wine bottles must be placed into a wine basket.

1. Place a napkin diagonally inside the wine basket with the front tip of the napkin slightly overlapping the end of the basket (where the neck of the bottle will sit)

2. From their horizontal storage at the "cave-du-jour" (label up), insert delicately (and still horizontally) the bottle into the wine basket.

3. Bring the basket to the table, without shaking it or having the bottle go vertically.

4. Place the neck of the basket over an upside-down saucer in order to raise the bottle slightly: during the uncorking process this will prevent the wine from overflowing onto the tablecloth.

To insure proper oxidation, red wine bottles (except the wines that will be decanted) should be opened 15-30 min. before serving.

OLD VINTAGE RED WINES *that do require decanting*

1. Have a guéridon *(serving table)* already placed next to the guests table

2. Have a candle on a saucer and a decanting carafe.

THE CORK

Once the wine is bottled, the producer must accomplish three steps, the corking, capsuling & labeling called "the bottle dress".

1. CORKING: Once the bottle is corked and capsuled, the cork allows the wine to breathe through it extremely slowly. Bottles corked with plastic corks must be avoided, as the wine will be jailed, unable to breath, thus killing the bouquet.

   The corks are washed and soaked in water before being squeezed and pressed into the neck of the bottle. With champagne & most of the sparkling bottles, the cork is larger than the other corks and enters half way into the bottle, then wired, giving it particular shape.

2. CAPSULE/CAP: Initially (and still used for "Grand Cru"), it was made of pewter and, consequently, defines how the capsule should be opened later. Mass production wines now use aluminum. The capsule is a straight cylinder that is dropped on top of the bottle. Then a machine goes over it and turns, making the capsule adhere to the bottle and giving it the same shape. This particular ring shape of the bottle was originally made to allow the capsule to stay.

3. LABEL: On some bottles, two labels are affixed: a small one on the top (usually for the vintage year) and a large one at the bottom. Notice at the bottom back of the bottle, opposite the label, there is an indentation: this allows the machine to know where to start gluing the labels.

UNCORKING

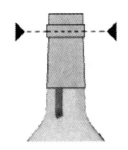

Holding the bottle at a slight angle, remove the top of the capsule by running the knife blade around the **middle** of the rim: *never above it (when pouring the wine, which will touch the capsule) or under (it will "undress" the bottle)* never put the capsule on the table!

Hold the bottle in your left hand above the label of the bottle. Insert the corkscrew inside the middle of the cork. Turn clockwise, the cork remaining still while the bottle turns.

Remove the cork and present it to the guest, on a saucer and on its right. Upon the guest's approval, the cork may be removed from the table

Wipe the neck of the bottle with the napkin to remove dust or sediment.

SERVING WHITE WINES

The two major types of white wine are:
- The sweet *(so called "dessert wines" such as Sauternes, Tokay, Hungarian Esszencia, etc., and*
- The dry that are served with savory dishes; the difference in serving these wines is only the two different temperatures that they are served, as explained on the previous page.

Preferably, white wines should be chilled 30-40 min. prior to serving in a wine ice bucket filled with ice cubes, water and a pinch of rock salt.

PRESENTING THE BOTTLE

Place the bottle into the ice bucket and carry the bucket to the table without shaking it.

- Place the ice bucket on its stand. *If an ice bucket stand is not available, place it on a plate at the end of the guest's table.*

- With a white napkin diagonally on your left hand, place the bottle, label up, and present it to the left of the guest for his or her approval.

- Return the bottle to the ice bucket.

POURING THE WINE

A cold or chilled bottle must not be handled with bare hands:

- Wrap it with a white napkin around the bottle diagonally, so the tip of the napkin is just below the neck of the bottle, covering the label, otherwise the wet label might slip away (and so will the bottle!)

- Starting with the guest who ordered, pour about 1 fl. oz in his or her glass. Step back and wait for the guest's approval. Serve the guests in the order described at the beginning of this chapter. Pour and fill up to 1/2 the glass.

It is always better to refill guest's glasses with fresh chilled wine.

Bring the bottle back to the ice bucket and wrap the napkin around it to keep the ice cube/water mix and the bottle cold.

The bottleneck must NEVER touch the rim of the glass!

SERVING SPARKLING WINES

Sparkling wines include: Champagne, Asti Spumante and other sparkling wines as well as ciders *(e.g., Cidre bouché from Normandy, France).*

Champagne is served in *flutes* or *tulip* glass, *never in a wide body glass, e.g. the "cup" style glass.*

Sparkling Wines are too often confused with Champagne: Champagne is a Province in France, northeast of Paris, where wine has been cultivated since the first century AD. Champagne growers copyrighted the name in the early 1900's. North America used the name prior to the copyright, so the U.S. is the **only** country in the world that is able to misuse it. Legend states that the "magic wine" was accidentally discovered in the late 1600's. It is the result of a double natural fermentation of a blend of Chardonnay, Pinot Noir & Pinot Meunier grapes. Originally a **red** wine, Champagne became a sweet white wine at Louis XIV's French Court, then a demi-sec, and a brut, early in the 1900's.

Presenting and pouring sparkling wines follows the same basic of white/rosé wines, to the exception that more precaution must be taken, as Champagne is bottled under great pressure; never shake the bottle!

PRESENTING THE BOTTLE

1. Place the bottle into the ice bucket and carry it to the table.
2. Place the ice bucket on its stand.

If an ice bucket stand is not available, place it on a plate on the table.

3. With a white napkin diagonally on your left hand, turn the bottle label up and present it to the left of the guest for his or her approval.

UNCORKING

A large majority of people is hesitant to open (uncork) sparkling bottles for the first time, because they are afraid of the pressure inside the bottle. It just takes a little practice and safety to stay in full control of this simple process if the following simple steps are taken:

The high pressure inside the bottle will eject any cork; to avoid this, a "wire cage" is put over it and twisted just below the neck's lip. Imprisoned, the cork is now secured.

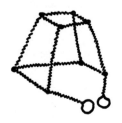

Uncork sparkling wine by removing this wire cage and removing the cork under your control, i.e. NO "POPS"

Return the bottle to the ice bucket and slant it to a 45^0 angle.

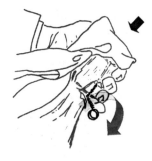

Away from the guests, find the round thumbnail of the wire muzzle and untwist it. Hold the napkin on your right hand (the thumb on top of the cork) and apply pressure.

Place your left hand at the bottom of the bottle and gently turn the ring clockwise with the right hand, the cork remaining still while the bottle turns. Do it slowly to avoid a "POP". You should hear a slight "HISS" sound as the cork exits the bottle. Present the cork to the guest, as you will with any other wine bottle.

POURING CHAMPAGNE

1. Wrap the bottle with the napkin and start with the guest who ordered.
2. Pour about 1 fl. oz in his or her glass.
3. Step back and wait for the guest's approval.
4. Serve the guests in the proper order described earlier.
5. Carefully pour a small quantity (to avoid the 'foam over' from the bubbles), filling up 2/3 of the glass)

Bring the bottle back to the ice bucket and wrap the napkin around it to keep the ice cube and the bottle cold.

When the bottle is empty, turn it upside down into the bucket: it shows that the bottle is really empty and signals the guest that he or she may order a new one.

NOTE: Contrary to popular belief, you should not "POP" open a bottle of Champagne.

SERVING RED WINES

Red wines are best served according to the temperature chart at the beginning of this chapter. Ideally, red wines should be opened about 1 hour before serving to allow a slow oxidation that will release its "bouquet".

PRESENTING THE BOTTLE

1. Bring a white napkin diagonally on your hand and forearm.

2. Place the bottle label up onto to the napkin.

3. Bending your body slightly, present it to the guest who ordered the bottle at his or her left side. Step back and wait for the guest's approval.

4. Remove the capsule foil and the cork as explained at the beginning of this chapter and wipe the rim to remove any dust or sediments.

POURING THE WINE

Red wines are served in a wide body glass. Each wine has its own glass shape, and should be used accordingly.

Put your hand over the label *(the bottle will stay on the table until empty)* Starting with the guest who ordered, pour about 1 fl. oz in his or her glass and wipe to top of the bottle to avoid any dripping on the tablecloth. Step back and wait for the guest's approval.

Serve the guests in the order described at the beginning of this chapter. Gently pour the glasses one by one.

Bring the bottle back to the table onto the small plate to avoid rings on the tablecloth.

PORT   OTHER RED WINE   GRAND BORDEAUX   BURGUNDY

SERVING WINES IN A BASKET

Old vintage red wines mostly contain sediments that are deposited on the opposite side of the label, as explained before. These wines are always placed into a wine basket.

See: WINE PREPARATION on BEFORE SERVING WINES, page 101

PRESENTING THE WINE

There are two ways to present this basket, depending on the location of the guest who ordered the wine:

1. If the guest is seated next to the end of the table, place the basket on your left hand and forearm, the neck of the bottle towards you.

2. If the guest is in between other guest's place the basket in your left hand only, the neck of the bottle away from you, so the guest will be able to see it.

UNCORKING THE WINE

The purpose of having the wine in a basket is because it has sediments. Therefore, the bottle must not be put straight up or turned during the uncorking process.

1. Leaving the basket on the table, cut the capsule by turning your hand around the neck of the bottle.

2. Remove the cork gently with the corkscrew. Wipe the neck of the bottle with the corner of your napkin. The whole process is done without removing the basket from the table.

POURING THE WINE

Place your right hand over the basket, and pour very gently into the glass.

Before removing the tip of the bottle from the glass, twist the bottle a few degrees so the drop does not fall on the tablecloth immediately.

Have a napkin on the other hand to wipe it immediately but discretely.

DECANTING

1. Have a lighted candle on a saucer in front of you.

2. With your left hand hold the carafe in a slight angle.

3. Hold the basket with your other hand perfectly level.

4. Place the neck of the bottle in front of the candlelight.

5. Very slowly pour the wine from the bottle into the carafe, constantly looking at the exit of the bottle.

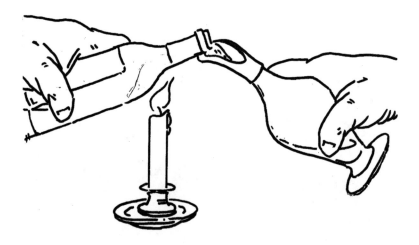

When the sediments start reaching the neck of the bottle, the decanting process is successfully done! Place the carafe back on the table.

THE IDEAL WINE TASTING GLASS

The glass is the ultimate tasting tool.

In order to help the tasting, the glass must both satisfy the eyes, the nose and the mouth requirement. With transparency, smoothness, and simplicity, it presents the wine at its best. It must not be too large, in order not to modify the wine's bouquet, although some Burgundy wines hold up in large glasses.

Its shape is oval, with a slightly narrow opening to concentrate the aromas. Its lip is thin to favor mouth contact. It has a stem, so the taster's hand does not transmit its warmth to the wine.

This glass, often called the "INAO glass" for "Institut National des Appellations d'Origine", is totally transparent and smooth; its semi-oval shape has a leg and a foot. It is made of crystalline glass, which contains about 9% lead.

Its total capacity is between 210 and 225 ml. (7-7.6 oz.), in which 70 to 80 ml. (2.4-2.7 oz.) is poured, or less than 1/3. This amount allows it to make a circular movement that helps to slowly develop the aromas with no risk of overflowing.

The Art of Hosting

CHAPTER 8

Serving Food

SERVING & CLEARING A TABLE

Serving guests and clearing their table during the course of their entire meal is a TEAM EFFORT. The slightest mistake by one of the wait staff reflects not only upon the rest of the team, but also the entire restaurant. How many times have you heard a guest on the way out saying, "I'll never come back, the server was so rude!" This remark may have been anyone besides the station team asking a question, a comment too abruptly and without finesse.

An unhappy guest means no decent tip that day, and an even lost future revenue from that specific guest (any most certainly from the guest's family, friends and acquaintances...)

To avoid these unfortunate situations, ALL wait staff, at every level, must follow the Rules of Serving Food & Drinks.

RULES OF SERVING

IN THE KITCHEN

- Place a cover over dishes in the kitchen.
- When cold & hot dishes are to be served at the same table, take cold food from the pantry first, then hot
- Hot food = hot plate; cold food = cold plate
- Make sure there is no food or sauce on the rim of the plate
- Keep thumb off the rim of the plate at all times
- Always use a tray to carry anything, whether you feel it is needed or not
- Side napkins (towels) may be used to serve hot plates

CARRYING A TRAY

- With your most comfortable arm, hold tray with one hand above your shoulder on flat of your palm (for heavy loads), or on the tips of your fingers (for light loads)
- Open swinging doors with opposite hand (not with foot)
- Always keep one hand free for protection from obstacles and quick recovery

SERVING A TABLE

- Bring condiments to the table prior to serving food
- Place silverware on the table *before* each course (make sure they are perfectly clean)
- Serve food plates from the left with the left hand
- Serve plates with entrée facing the guest
- Serve beverages from the right with the right hand

CLEARING A TABLE

- When ALL guests at the table are done with one dish (and ONLY then), clear the plate from the right with the right hand: *"May I take this for you?"*
- When serving two wines (one for the appetizer, the second for entrée), and when the wine is done, clear the glass from the right with the right hand
- Before dessert is to be served, crumb the table (after all plates, utensils and condiments are removed)

CLEARING THE TABLE ONTO A TRAY

- Place *tray jack* (collapsible, portable table stand) and lined tray away from the table
- Never bus items onto a tray holding food to be served
- Clear plates (ladies first) from the right
- Place the first plate on the tray as a scrap plate
- Scrape off all other plates onto it
- Stack the plates and cover with the scrap plate
- Clear all beverage glasses that are finished and place in the center of the tray (never put your fingers inside the glasses)
- Never put more than two coffee cups on top of each other
- Clear all side dishes, bread & butter plates and utensils that will not be needed for the following course
- Place all silverware in one location on the side of the tray, all facing the same direction
- Carry the well-balanced tray
- Pick up the tray jack with the other hand
- Carry the tray and the tray jack through the dining room
- Place the tray jack at its pick-up location
- Bring the tray to the dishwashing area
- Trash the contents of the scrap plate
- Stack plates onto the dishwashing countertop
- Gently drop the silverware into the container filled with detergent without splashing
- Place glasses and coffee cups in their proper racks

DIFFERENT TYPES OF SERVICE

Although the most common way to serve food nowadays is by the plate, one should know that according of the class of the restaurant, special event, home dinner service or tableside, it might not be always the case.

According to the required style of service, the wait staff is more or less involved. Following are the different types of service:

- French (served on a dish)
- English (served on a dish)
- Russian (served on a dish)
- On the tableside cart (served either on a dish or by the plate)
- By the plate

FRENCH / *SERVICE À LA FRANÇAISE*

This service is most common at a home sit-down dinner, whereas the guest picks up the food that he or she likes (instead of having the plate with food that guests may not like); *Home sit-down dinners do not have a menu to choose from!*

The food is placed on a dish in the kitchen and brought to the table. The butler then presents the dish, which has a large spoon and fork on it (handle facing the guest) to each guest.

ENGLISH / *SERVICE À L'ANGLAISE*

Used in banquet service for practical purposes: it is easier for the kitchen to place several servings on a large dish than serving food on each individual plate.

The waiter brings the dish to his banquet station and serves in the order the guests are seated. Serving the food with the right hand, the service is done from the left of the guest.

This service resembles the French service, as each guest is able to speak to the waiter to avoid any food of his or her disliking.

RUSSIAN / *SERVICE À LA RUSSE*

This is a service that is less and less in practice. It consists of serving food from a dish in the waiter station. It is still in use in some Brasseries, where a serving cart is not feasible, as there is not enough room in between tables to use a cart to serve tableside.

TABLESIDE CART / *SERVICE AU GUÉRIDON*

Also called "guéridon", this service consists of receiving food in a plate or large dish that the food runner brings to the cart with the appropriate number of plates (hot or cold according to the nature of the dish). The captain then brings the food from the dish to the plate, duplicating the dish decoration on the plate.

This service is used principally nowadays when a flambéing and carving process is required tableside.

Just a few examples: a large food assortment tray (cheeses, antipasti, pâtés, etc.) that cannot be served or placed on the guests' table, any dish that needs a carving process (rack of lamb, chateaubriand), desserts such as Cherries Jubilee, Bananas Foster, coffee cocktails, etc.)

BY THE PLATE / *SERVICE À L'ASSIETTE*

This service allows the Chef to present the plate with its own creative decoration, being sure that it will not be misrepresented by accident or by an unprofessional wait staff member.

It is more convenient for the wait staff, as no extra work is necessary and is done properly as long as the entrée is placed facing the guest.

SERVING BREAD

Bread must be considered a food, just like appetizers, entrees and others. Although it is the only "free food" on any menu, it is the first food served to the guest. Therefore it must be served appropriately with the garnishes that the house offers.

TYPES OF BREAD

Bread can be homemade or purchased, and can be served from room temperature to hot. When served hot, it must be wrapped in a napkin to keep it hot and served at once. One type of bread may be served, or a combination of them.

Here are some types of bread:

DRY : Biscottes, dry bread sticks, crackers
SOFT: French baguette, sourdough rolls, croissants, soft dinner rolls, Facaccia, toasted bread, etc.

GARNISHES

Bread is never served by itself, but rather with garnishes that must be served at the same time:

- ❖ Butter in any form (wrapped or not, whipped) must be cold but not hard
- ❖ Roasted garlic (cold, warm or hot)
- ❖ Humus
- ❖ Olives
- ❖ Pâtés

These garnishes are always placed in the center of the table in order to be easily accessible to each guest.

BREAD SERVED ON THE BREAD PLATE

This type of service belongs to the fine restaurant, where elegant service is absolute and no short cuts are allowed. It is served at the same time as the appetizer *(not before)*. It is wrapped in a white napkin and brought to the table in a basket.
Form a tong using a large fork and spoon as shown below. Serve the bread to the left side of the guest onto the bread plate.

SERVICE

In all other restaurants, bread is served immediately when the guests sit down. This practice allows guests to have a first free course and subsequently order less food.

Served in a basket, on a wooden board or other type of container, it is placed in the center of the table. (*When hot, wrap it in a napkin*)

Bread, the bread container <u>and</u> breadcrumbs must be removed before serving dessert, either with a clean folded napkin or a long metal breadcrumber.

SERVING SOUPS

Soup is the first course on any given menu. It may sometimes wrongly be considered an appetizer (when offered with a choice of house salad).

When food is ordered, serve the soup in the proper container *immediately,* while the kitchen staff starts cooking the appetizer/entrées. Soups are always made in advance and are available without a wait time.

TYPES OF SOUP

Soups can be made COLD or HOT:
- COLD: Vichyssoise, Gazpacho, jellied consommés. Cold soups **must** be served **CHILLED** and poured into the appropriate **CHILLED** container. *A chilled soup in a warm container? Just think about it!*
- HOT: Veloutés, chowder, creams or soups *(e.g.: French onion soup, minestrone, any broth containing a solid element).*

Hot soups must be served in a warm or lukewarm container, NEVER in a chilled container!

CUP OF SOUP

Family-style restaurants some-times offer a cup of soup as part of a fixed price menu or it can be included in the price of the entrée. Using a ladle, pour the soup up to ½ in. to the rim. Clean any spillage before placing onto a saucer. Place the cup/saucer onto a dessert plate (underliner) topped with a doily. Place a small soupspoon on the underliner. Bring the soup on a tray to the guest at once.

BOWL OF SOUP

Bowl soup is usually served "à la Carte". The right way to serve a bowl of soup is **tableside** from a soup dish, or "Soupière"; it reduces spillage and ensures a hot temperature. Place the bowl onto a large plate (underliner) covered by a small napkin. It helps keep the bowl on its underliner and absorbs any spillage).

Never place the soupspoon onto the underliner; it should already be on the table, at the extreme right of the large knife.

SERVED FROM A SOUP DISH

When soup comes from the kitchen in a large soup dish, use a large ladle. *Mainly used at tableside service or in banquets.*

- Dip into the container and fill the ladle up to 2/3 and lift out of the soup.

- Go back down just so the bottom of the ladle touches the soup, and serve immediately into the guest's soup plate.

This keeps the soup from dropping down while carrying the ladle!

SOUP GARNISHES

Some soups require garnishes (spices, croutons, cheese, etc.) They must be brought to the guest at the same time as the soup; using a spoon, offer them to the guest and place the plate with remaining garnish to the right of the guest (at the opposite side of the bread plate).

If cheese is part of the garnishes and is already grated, it should be offered to the guest.

When using a block of cheese (Parmesan, Gruyère, etc.) use a cheese grater and offer it to the guest, grating from the guest's right side.

The Art of Hosting

SERVING APPETIZERS

Appetizer means: *"to excite the appetite"*. Served in smaller portions than the entrées, and after the soup, it is normally the second course of the meal in a gala dinner.

As always, use an underliner when serving appetizers.

COLD APPETIZERS

There is a large variety of cold appetizers, including Antipasti, Shellfish (Shrimp Cocktail), crustaceans on a half shell, Pâtés & Mousses, Caviar, Cold Cuts, etc.

Some appetizers require special silverware (*see TABLE SET-UP: SILVERWARE, page 27*). These utensils must be on the table *before* bringing the appetizers out.

SALADS

Part of the cold appetizers, they are sometimes considered entrées, especially at lunchtime. More elaborate than the House Salad, they are prepared at the pantry kitchen station. Although they usually do not require special garnishes, additional pepper and grated cheese must be offered to the guest at the table.

Cold appetizers (just like the hot appetizers) must be served at once, so they are served at the proper temperature.

THE OTHER SALADS

HOUSE SALAD: family restaurants include this salad in their menu/entrée price (just like bread and butter) to attract their clientele.

Offer the choice of dressings, if it will be tossed or served on the side (in a soufflé cup or a monkey dish on a saucer with doily). When served, offer pepper (from the peppermill) to be served at the right side of the guest.

HOT APPETIZERS

All hot appetizers require cooking time from 5-15 min. Order them at once from the kitchen, even if you do not have the entrees ordered yet.

Place the appropriate silverware on the table for each guest prior to serving. Only when the hot appetizers for the table are ready to be picked up in the kitchen should you then pick up the cold ones and bring them to the table.

SERVING SAUCES

When sauce is ordered or just served "on the side", it is first poured into a "Gooseneck" (also called "sauceboat"). As with any china, use a cold sauceboat for cold sauce, hot sauceboat for hot sauce, lukewarm sauceboat for lukewarm sauce (e.g., hollandaise sauce).

Unless already part of saucer, the sauceboat is placed on a saucer topped with a doily and a small spoon on the side. Since it is part of the dish, the sauceboat must be brought to the guests' table together with the food.

After the plate is placed in front of the guest, **from the right side** of the guest, offer to pour some of the sauce over the main ingredient.

After served, place the sauceboat on its saucer and spoon on the right of the guest.

When serving melted butter, first light up the heating source for the butter melting equipment and then place it on the guest's right side. Only then the container filled with the melted butter is placed over the melter equipment.

Melted butter is never poured over the dish by the Captain, but is the guest's privilege to dip the food into it.

NOTE: Sauces, although part of side orders, are NOT placed on the left side of the guest, but on the right side as explained in the next chapter.

SERVING SIDE ORDERS

By definition, side orders are not placed on the main dish plate by the Chef, therefore, are not to be served onto the plate by any wait staff!

Side orders can be bread (bread plate), garnishes, starches (rice, potato, etc.), salads or vegetables, which are brought to the guest's table along with the main dish plate.

Only after the main dish plate has been placed in front of the guest is the side-order dish placed on the **left** of the guest.

Some side dishes require additional silverware, which must be on the table prior to placing the side order on the table. Below are some examples of needed dessert silverware:

SPOON — For a side order of Chili: place on the saucer (topped with a doily) on the right side and at a 45^0 angle, handle facing the guest.

KNIFE — For bread: set at a 45^0 angle slightly on the upper side of the bread plate, handle facing the guest)

Side orders are placed on the left side of the guest.

SERVING SEAFOOD

Seafood includes both fish and crustaceans. However they are cooked, head, fins, bones and skin must be removed prior to serving them to the guests. This is done by using a large spoon and fork—never bare hands! Have a hot, clean plate on which the filleted fish will be placed and served to the guest.

WHOLE FISH

Most fish served today is already filleted, skinned and dressed on the plate with sauce and garnishes. It does not require special work from the wait staff. For sauce serving, refer to the previous chapter.

European and Asian restaurants often serve their portion size fish WHOLE: (cooking fish with the skin on holds in moisture, and the bones impart more flavor (after all fish stock/bouillon is made from bones!). These fish are sautéed ("meunière" type), grilled, poached (Cioppino or Bouillabaisse type), steamed, fried or in "papillote". Whatever the recipe, whole fish are de-boned tableside: it's quite a show, and quite a treat!

There are two major categories of fish: round and flat. They are not exactly carved the same way, as round fish have two filets while flatfish have four.

FLATFISH

Flatfishes include flounder, turbot, sole and Dover sole.

Wider or narrower, they basically all have the same shape as shown. Flatfishes are very lean, as most of them contain less than 1 - 1.4% fat!

FILETING FLATFISH

Removing the bones differs according to how the fish was sautéed or grilled:
- Sautéed fish has a crusty skin. It should stay on the filet, unless the guest asks for it to be removed: Gently scrape it from head to tail and discard.
- Grilled fish has a nice grill marking that should be served showing it. Therefore the top filet is never split!

HEAD

With the large spoon, cut off the head just behind the gill plate and all around it. Place it on the discard plate.

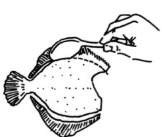
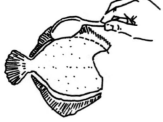

FINS

With the spoon, push the fin away from the filet little by little, gently derooting the fins from the fish. Place on the discard plate.

TOP FILETS

Place the spoon under the top filets, against the bones, and slide the spoon gently from the head to the tail. Using the fork, cut the filet from the tail.

GRILLED TOP FILET

Using both the spoon and the fork, lift the two filets (kept attached) and place in the center of the plate, top side up.

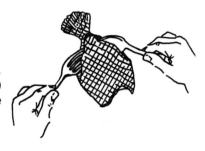

DE-BONING

Holding the fish with the fork, place the spoon just underneath the bones and slide toward the tail, separating the bones from the bottom. Discard the bones onto the side plate.

BOTTOM FILETS

Make a slit along the back center, separating the two bottom filets.

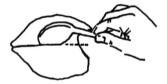

THE SERVING PLATE

Place on the guest's plate, on each side of the top filet.

ROUND FISH

Round fish include trout and snapper. Filleting round fish is easier and faster than flatfish, as round fish have only two filets, which are slightly thicker.

The following round fish process applies for round fish in "Papillote", after the wrapper poach has been opened by inserting one tooth of the fork into the wrapper and gently tearing it to expose the fish.

TOP FILET

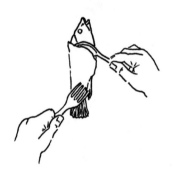

Place the fish head away from you, the tail towards you. With the edge of the large spoon, make a slit along the back of the fish, from the tail to the head; this separates the top filet from the bottom filet. After the top filet is separated from the bones, using the spoon and the fork, lift it to the side of the plate.

DE-BONING

Place the spoon underneath the tailbone, between the bone and the bottom filet. Making a slight waving movement, go toward the head. Remove the bone and head to the discard plate.

SERVING THE FILLETS

With the fork & spoon, lift the bottom filet to the serving plate. Place the top filet on top of the bottom filet. *The serving plate should already have the vegetables & starch on it.*

SHELLING LOBSTER

Unlike all other fish, all shellfish have their bone outside their flesh. In fine dining establishments, shelling a lobster is a must!

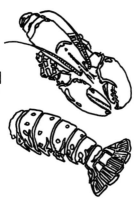

Shellfish [Maine Lobster, Caribbean Rock (Spiny) Lobster] usually come already opened, claws split or cracked from the kitchen.

If it is not the case, or upon guest's request, the shell must obviously be opened, cracked or removed by the Captain.

TOOLS

- Cutting board
- Nutcracker
- Cocktail fork
- Sharp knife

- Large fork
- Several clean napkins
- Medium size bowl
  (*for discards*)

MAINE LOBSTER

This is probably the most common shellfish that guests require to be shelled. According to the moulting season, Maine Lobsters can have a soft or a hard shell (or anywhere in between).

In any case, although the shell will be discarded and not served to the guests, this is food, and must never be touched by bare hands! Clean white napkins are the gloves of the Captain: it avoids direct contact with the food, as well as protecting hands, so use them!

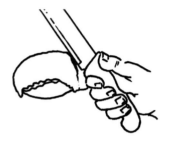

CLAWS

- Tear-off the claws from the head and the claw from the knuckle

- Place the claw on the cutting board

- Hold it on the side with the left hand and make a quick dent on the edge of the claw (*see left drawing*)

- Split the claw in half

- Remove the claw meat with the cocktail fork if necessary

CLAW KNUCLES

Using the nutcracker and the cocktail fork, remove the inside of the remainder of the leg.

TAIL

- Separate the tail by twisting the body from the tail.

- Turn the tail bottom side up. Using scissors (or the knife) cut each side of the soft bottom shell. (*see page 151*)

- Remove the soft shell and discard.

- Insert the fork teeth at the tail side, between the shell and the tail flesh.

- With a slight criss-cross movement, go toward the opposite side, removing the tail flesh from its shell.

- Cut the fantail and set aside.

- Discard the shell and place the tail flesh on the cutting board.

- Cut the tail into medallions at a slight angle, starting from the fantail. (*see page 141*)

LEGS

- Remove the legs from the body.

- Crack the joint and pull the flesh, one leg at a time.

- With the nutcracker, open the knuckle and remove the flesh with the cocktail fork.

- Discard the gills in the bowl.

SERVING THE LOBSTER

Reconstitute the lobster on the serving plate:

- Place the body upside-down.

- Fill the body with parsley (salad) and top with the lobster pieces.

- Place the medallions below the body, and the fantail below.

- Fan the legs on each side of the body.

- Place the claws on each side of the body.

When serving SHELLFISH, the following must be given to the guest before the serving plate is placed in front of them:

- Place a "bib" or white napkin around the guest's neck.

- Place a nutcracker and cocktail fork on the right, outside the large knife.

- Butter melter or sauce (on a saucer topped with a doily, a coffee spoon on the side) placed on the right of the guest.

A fingerbowl or wet napkin topped with lemon quarters on a dessert plate is placed next to the bread plate. Replace it if used frequently.

ROCK LOSTER TAIL

It is very doubtful that a Rock Lobster tail will be served whole from the kitchen. They are usually served either butterflied (*picture at left*) or split lengthwise. *If served whole, the process is the same as for the Maine Lobster.*

There are two ways to remove the meat from the lobster tail:

1. Splitting the lobster tail in half, and then removing the meat from the two halves,
2. Cutting the back (softer) shell and then removing the whole lobster tail meat. This certainly the best, but rather unknown way, as the meat is then sliced into medallions that are nicely aligned on top of the shell.

1. SPLITTING THE TAIL IN HALF

With a napkin, hold the fantail with the left hand.
Plunge the fork teeth into the end of the tail meat.
Rotate your wrist: the meat will separate from the shell

REMOVING THE TAIL MEAT

Hold the shell with the left hand (*wrapped in a clean napkin*).
Place a fork firmly in the meat (*fan tail side*) and twist your wrist; this process separates the meat from the shell easily.

2. THE WHOLE LOBSTER TAIL

Place the whole lobster tail upside down on the cutting board.
Using a sharp knife (or a pair of scissors) cut each side of the bottom soft shell.
Place a fork firmly in the meat (*fan tail side*) and lift up to remove the meat from its shell.

THE MEDALLIONS

Cut the tail meat diagonally into medallions as shown on the right.

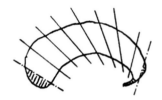

SERVING & PRESENTATION

Place the shell upside up on the serving plate.
Starting from the fantail, place the medallions, well-aligned, into the shell.

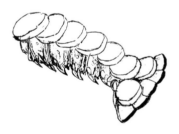

SERVING PASTA

Pastas are best served in a bowl-type plate over an underliner topped with a doily. Place a large spoon on the right of the guest's knife. Just like soups, the bowl must never be touched.

> RULE: Remember: always serve dishes from the **left** side of the guest.

Offer to grate some cheese over the guest's pasta (best cheeses are: Parmesan-Reggiano or Romano)

> RULE: Grate the cheese from the **right** side of the guest.

Olive oil must be present on the table. It is placed on a saucer to avoid oil dripping on the table (with tablecloth or not).

Additional silverware includes a large spoon placed on the right side, next to the large knife, used as a support for rolling the pasta.

SERVING MEAT

When the meat is placed on one side of the plate and vegetables & starches on the other. Always place the meat close to the guest. Prior to serving the dish, place the steak knife at the right of the guest.

SERVING SKEWER

With a clean napkin, hold one end of the skewer with the left hand (*if the skewer is metallic, chances are it is burning hot!*).

Raise this end to a 45^0 angle.

Insert the middle tooth in between the second or third piece of meat.

Firmly remove the first two or three pieces of meat from the skewer by pulling the end of the skewer (left hand).

Repeat until all pieces are removed.

Arrange all pieces on the serving plate to reconstitute the skewer shape (i.e., give the skewer pieces the same shape and alignment that it had on the skewer)

CARVING

The purpose of this book is not to go through an entire carving and flambéing review process; this, by itself, would be the subject of another book.

Here are the most common meats that need light carving before serving: Rack of Lamb and Chateaubriand.

Just like filleting fish or de-boning lobster, the meats that need preparation must be brought to the table first (before the rest of the other guests' food is served to avoid its being cold) and presented to the guest. Once carved, the rest of the dishes must brought to the table and all dishes served at the same time.

RACK OF LAMB

Rack of Lamb is usually served for one order. When cut properly, the rack gives four chops, as it is cut at every other bone, making even cuts.
One bone on each chop is then removed, giving the impression of a nice, thick chop.

CUTTING THE CHOPS

- With a large fork and spoon, bring the rack onto the cutting board.
- Holding the rack with a large fork, cut between the second and third bones.
- Repeat cuts on every other bone. The last chop must be on the widest part of the loin.

- Bring the chop upward by using the fork.
- Starting from the top, place the knife against one bone at an angle.
- Cut down to remove the bone with no meat attached.

Repeat with the other chops.

- Place the chops onto the serving plate in a criss-cross manner on the opposite side of the garnishes (starch & vegetables).

CHATEAUBRIAND

Chateaubriand and London Broil are part of the trimmed and cleaned muscles, making it easier to show the long fiber lines called "grain". Slicing these muscles consists of cutting in the opposite direction of the fibers; this is called "against the grain".
Slice the meat at approximately 30^0 angle (against the grain) in order to be more tender. The slices are then placed onto the serving plate in a fan shape.

RULE: Place the fork upside down (never pick into the meat, which will make it bleed)

Cut slices from one end of the meat to the last, always keeping the knife at approximately 30^0 angle.

SERVING CHEESE

In North America, cheeses may be served as hors d'oeuvres at a cocktail party. They are usually served with fresh fruits, crackers, bread, butter and garnishes, including whole cumin (for imported Munster), etc. In Europe it is served after the salad (which is served after the entrée). Cheese should be removed from the fridge at least an hour before serving to allow it to come to room temperature.

This service may be found in some fine dining European restaurants.

- Before serving cheese, bring more fresh bread
- Bring some butter (not chilled)
- Bring a clean fork (left) and knife (right) to the guest.

SERVICE

1. Cheese assortments are served just as any other dish, in the kitchen at the pantry station (on a cold plate). The cheese plate should include 3-5 different cheeses. It should be garnished with washed cut fresh fruits and some nuts (nuts enhance both the cheese and the wine served with them). The plate is served with the left hand at the left side of the guest.

2. When served from a small tray (small selection), a few steps must be followed:

   - Place a dessert plate in front of the guest
   - Make a "tong" with a fork and a knife (both of the same large size) *see page 124*
   - Place the tray over the left hand
   - From the **right** with the **right** hand, cut each guest's cheese choice and make the tong to serve each cheese onto the guest's plate

3. When cheeses are on a large tray (on serving cart):

- Bring the cart to the right of the guest
- Place a dessert plate on the cart (next to the tray)
- Serve the cheese from the cart
- When the guest's choice is done, serve on the **right** with the **right** hand, using a knife and a fork.

RULE: Just like sauces, serving grated cheese, cheeses are served from the guest's right side to avoid bringing your elbow too close of the guest's face.

Back, from left to right: Blue cheese, Gruyère
Front, from left to right: ash goat cheese, Camembert, herbed rolled Goat cheese

SERVING DESSERT

Selling desserts is always a controversy among wait staff and it shouldn't be. In Europe desserts are an absolute part of the meal, no questions asked! The palate needs some sweets at the end of a meal; therefore desserts are very much sellable, just like any other dish. After all, the dessert menu is never limited to fat desserts, but also includes ice cream, sherbet/sorbet, and some type of fresh fruit. And don't be afraid to suggest that the guests share. *Some restaurants even have a sampling dessert plate, where a small portion of the dessert menu is offered for that purpose.*

Desserts include:
- Cakes, pies and tarts (cold, hot or lukewarm)
- Ice cream and sherbet/sorbet (plain or in a composition)
- Fruits (plain, in salad form or in combination with the above)
- Desserts prepared tableside, using some carving and/or flambéing

As with all other dishes, desserts are served with the left hand to the left side of the guest.

THE FRAME OF MIND

So many times I've heard waiters say, "Desserts are too difficult to sell. My guests are now full and don't want to eat something else…"

With that in mind, no wonder why you cannot sell desserts! A professional will, and, with a few tips, you will be able to do exactly the same.

When you have friends or family for dinner in your house, don't you have a dessert (cake, pie or tart), ice cream or a basket of fresh fruits at the end of the meal? Shouldn't the same apply in a restaurant? Of course!

Now, more than ever, it's crucial to remember that you do not only wait on tables, but you are also a salesperson (keep in mind the gratuities!).

SELLING TIPS

After the table has been cleared, tablecloth crumbed, unnecessary glasses, condiments, etc. removed, now it's time to show off.

In addition to those described earlier ("SELLING THE ORDER" chapter, page 69), the following are some more winning tips:

- If a dessert cart is not available, and whenever possible, have a silver tray with a sampling of cakes, tarts and pies.

- Describe all desserts displayed on the tray/cart, such as: "Here we have a fresh fruit tart baked in a mini piecrust with vanilla filling, etc. (*describe* all desserts).

- Immediately after, talk about "diet" desserts not on the tray/cart, such as:
  " ... and last but not least, for those on a special diet we offer fresh strawberries and pineapple dipped in white and dark chocolate or plain with or without ice cream/sorbet or Chantilly cream. Now which one would you like?"

- If fresh fruits are available, offer to carve (peel them tableside) *It is simple, but it is always a winner.*

- When tableside desserts are on the menu, such as flambé desserts (Bananas Foster, Cherries Jubilee, Baked Alaska), Sabayon, etc. are on the menu, they should be offered first.

You will be amazed at the results, after all, who can resist?

The goal is to sell your most extraordinary dessert at the first table reaching the dessert point.

To illustrate the above, a little true story about what I used to do in my own restaurants:

When dessert time was coming, I used to give a busboy or food runner a Baked Alaska and told him to go in the dining room and get lost. This was a way to show every single table how beautiful the Baked Alaska was and put them in the mood for it. It always worked without failure; the large majority of tables said: what is that? And half of the tables ordered it.

DESSERTS WITH SAUCES

For all entrees served with sauces:

- Bring the sauce in a sauceboat on top of a saucer covered with a doily

- Serve them on the right side of the guest and leave the sauceboat on the right of the guest

TABLESIDE PEELING TECHNIQUES

Fresh fruits can be of one kind or an assortment of several to make a salad-type plate. This process used to be very common at the beginning of the 20th century and is rarely in practice today.

As the fruits cannot be touched with hands, it requires a cutting board, large fork and a sharp knife. All fruits are not "carved" the same way, as explained below.

CITRUS FRUITS

1. Cut each end of the fruit by plunging the fork on one end to hold it.
2. Repeat on the other hand.
3. Place one flat side on the cutting board.
4. Placing the fork in the center of the fruit, cut the peel all the way around it.
5. Cut the fruit in slices that are then fanned on the plate.

APPLE & PEAR

1. Apply the same two-step process as for the citrus.
2. Cut in quarters.
3. Holding the quarter with the fork, remove the core.
4. Cut each quarter in half and place on the serving plate.

BANANA

1. Put the banana on the cutting board.
2. Hold the banana with the curved side of the fork and cut one end.
3. Hold the banana with second fork at the opposite end, with the left hand.
4. Pierce one tooth of the fork into the skin and above the banana meat at the opposite end.
5. Go straight to the cut end.
6. Repeat several times until the entire peel is removed.

FIGS

It is basically the same process as the banana.
1. Cut any end.
2. Hold the fig upward with a fork.
3. Pierce the fig skin with another fork's tooth and pull upward. Repeat until the peel is removed.

With these basic techniques, you will be able to prepare most of fresh fruits by adapting them to a specific fruit.

FLAMBEING DESSERT

Only a well-trained Captain should do these desserts, as any mishandling of alcohol may cause severe injuries. They require a tableside cart, a gas stove, a copper pan, a large spoon and a fork. All ingredients are placed on the side of the cart along with the serving plates.

Here are two examples:

BANANAS FOSTER

Peel and slice the banana, as explained above.

In the heated copper pan, spoon some butter and let it melt.
Spoon brown sugar and cinnamon and turn it in the pan.
Hold a lime quarter with the fork teeth and turn until the sugar is totally melted.

Bring the banana slices onto the pan and sauté a few minutes, turning occasionally until they are slightly cooked.
Flambé with dark rum and serve over vanilla ice cream.

CHERRIES JUBILEE

Same as above, but with white sugar, and no cinnamon. Flambé with cherry brandy.

CHAPTER 9

Other Services

The Ashtray

Presenting the Check

Resetting Tables

THE ASHTRAY

When a smoking section is still available for guests, one must know how to serve matches and handle the ashtrays.

MATCHES

When a personalized matchbox (with the establishment's logo printed on the cover) it must be presented and set in the center of the ashtray. There are two kinds of matchboxes that are presented differently:

1. The matchbook is open with the cover behind top of the matches

2. The match box is slightly open with two matches going over (outside)

When the astray is already in the center of the table, these matchboxes must be placed inside the clean ashtray.

If requested by the guest, the matchbox (or cigarettes with matches) is presented on its left side on a small underliner.

THE ASHTRAY

After two cigarette butts (and no more!) have been extinguished in the ashtray, it must be removed by putting a small saucer (or another ashtray) over the dirty one, while you replace it with a clean one with the other hand.

PRESENTING THE CHECK

This is the moment where wait staff member may destroy all the good work done during the guests' dining experience.

The check can only be "served" to the guest when the guest (who obviously will pay the bill) asks for it.

Giving the check to the table before being requested by a guest give the guest the clear message:

> "Pay **now** and leave, because I need the table!"

When guests are suspected not to order anything else, just request:
> "Is there anything else you wish to order?"

Only then, prepare the check and review the ordered items to avoid repeats or mistakes. Place the check into a clean check presenter and place it in your wait station, ready to be "served" to the guest. Have ready after dinner mints or cookies that the house offers; place them on a saucer topped with a doily.

When the check is requested, place it on a dessert plate and "serve" it immediately on the left of the paying guest. After the guest places his payment inside the check holder, remove it and perform that payment either by processing a credit card or cash (personal or company checks are rarely accepted as less secure for payment). When a credit card is used, return the check holder (for credit card payment, bring a clean working pen. After the guest has placed his or her credit card, bring it back for processing and bring it back to the guest for signature)

Upon guests' departure, help ladies by moving chairs away so it is easier to stand. Accompany guests to the door.

Return to the table and check around and below it for forgotten guest belongings and reset the table.

RESETTING TABLES

Once the guests have left, resetting the table is often crucial, as it might be needed for other guests with or without reservation. The table must look like no one used it before.

1. Remove all remaining dishes from the table onto a tray on its tray jack, placing glasses in the center of the tray, as explained on page 120.

2. Top the tray with the tablecloth gently folded. This insures stability while bringing the tray to the dishwashing area.

3. Using a napkin, dust each chair to remove any breadcrumbs or other foreign objects.

4. Clean the floor around and underneath the table using a small broom or a "Bissell" type broom.

5. Reset the table.

If any belongings were left after the guests' departure, bring them back to the hostess at the front desk, along with a piece of paper with:

- Your name
- Date
- Shift
- Table number

so the guests' name can be compared to the reservation chart & telephone number and contacted.

CHAPTER 10

Appendix

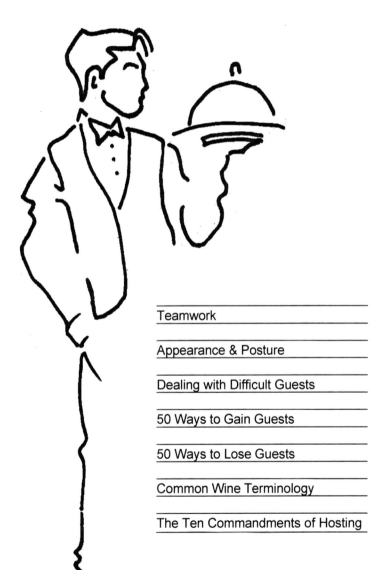

Teamwork

Appearance & Posture

Dealing with Difficult Guests

50 Ways to Gain Guests

50 Ways to Lose Guests

Common Wine Terminology

The Ten Commandments of Hosting

The Art of Hosting

TEAMWORK

The restaurant business resembles a symphonic orchestra: if any musician makes a wrong note, starts too early or too late, it affects the whole harmony.

It is absolutely a team effort! One of the most important ingredients in a pleasant dining experience is the frame of mind of the team, therefore the frame of mind of the person on the serving end. A positive frame of mind is extremely important. After all, cheerfulness and helping each other is contagious.

- Cooperate with the management and stand in unison with their goals and philosophies
- Respect your coworkers, and help them when possible; you'll appreciate it when your turn comes!

Here are some suggestions to help you increase your value to the restaurant and gain respect from everyone:

1. Don't be critical of your fellow employees.
2. Take pride in the excellence of your work.
3. Always do more than expected
4. Never adopt the attitude "Let someone else worry about it ... that's not my job!"
5. Take instructions and recommendations willingly and obey all rules.
6. Don't let someone else's poor work or negative attitude affect you; be enthusiastic, enjoy your work!
7. Continue to strive for self-improvement. After all, one learns something new every day.
8. Do not take part in rumors and gossip about any coworker.

APPEARANCE & POSTURE

Below are the basic rules that all wait staff must follow at all times.

1.	Arrive at work on time, i.e. five (5) minutes before your shift time.
2.	Upon arrival acknowledge your supervisors to make your presence noticed.
3.	Arrive at work well groomed and fully dressed in your uniform.
4.	Uniforms must be **clean** and **starched** or **ironed**.
5.	Always carry your working tools: pen, breadcrumber, cork opener, small flashlight, order book, etc.
6.	Bad breath and body odor are very offensive in food service, so personal hygiene is very important: • You should practice good hygiene by bathing daily. • Keep your hair neat and clean, and use deodorant/ antiperspirant.
7.	Hands and fingernails must be kept clean, trimmed and manicured. *Clear or neutral nail polish only.*
8.	Men: • Be clean-cut and shaven. • Beards are not acceptable. • Use absolutely no perfumes, colognes or scented after-shaves. • Use neither earrings nor visible body piercing.
9.	Ladies: • Have hair pulled back or up, with no loose ends. • Do not wear dangle earrings. • Do not wear objects and bows in hair; *small barrettes are permitted.* • Wear a minimum amount of make-up so it looks natural.
10.	Pins and broaches are not part of the uniform.
11.	More than one ring on each hand is not permissible.

12. Costume jewelry is not permissible.

13. Shoes must be freshly polished

14. Keep hands out of pockets, apron, etc.

15. Hands must be washed after using bathroom or smoking.

16. Do not lean on walls, counters, tables, chairs, bar rails, etc

17. Always maintain a professional stance, never slouching or squatting.

18. Always appear **idle** at any time

19. ALWAYS SMILE: leave your personal problems outside your work place.

20. All wait staff must remain in complete uniform while on duty during their whole shift.

21. Upon departure, let your supervisor know that you are leaving.

DEALING WITH DIFFICULT GUESTS

The restaurant business is an integral part of the Hospitability Industry:

> Hospitable [hos'pitebl] *adj*: welcoming, friendly, warm, open, generous, kind cordial, sociable

Anyone who doesn't have these basic qualities has NO business in this respectable and honorable industry! **Period!**

This point being made, as a service industry dealing with the general public, unhappy faces and characters are inevitable. Although it is not always pleasant, one has to deal with it in a courteous manner, and in a gentle way, make the grumpiest guest have the happiest meal that he or she has had for a long time. It is not always easy, but here are some tips that can help:

- The Early Guests — Always come a few minutes before the restaurant opens! Receive them courteously and explain when the service will begin; suggest they to go to the bar, or give them a comfortable seat, the menu and offer to take a drink order while they wait (if the bar is open).

- The Late Guests — These are the people that nobody wants, right? Most often, these are the best guests that you will have! *They usually are wine drinkers and generous tipper.*

163

Make them feel welcome. When the food selection is limited, explain that it is near closing time. Endeavor to provide good service without making them feel that they are being hurried.

- The Hurried Guests

They want to be in and out. Recommend ready items (most of the time, the specials), items that do not require a long time to cook. Always tell them in advance about how long the service will take. Give the best service under the circumstances.

- The Tired Guests

They come to the restaurant to relax and need a quiet place, definitely away from any sources of noise. Serve them quietly. A good tip is to suggest a hot soup or appetizing light food, or a hot drink in cold weather. On a hot day, suggest a chilled salad or a frosted drink.

- The Over Familiar Guests

Avoid playing their game at all cost: be courteous but dignified with them. Avoid long conversations and stay away from the table except when actual service is needed.

Now the most challenging guests: the Grouchy, Angry and Troublemakers. In all of these cases, NOTIFY the management at once, and then your coworkers.

- The Grouchy Guests

  Greet them cheerfully and serve them pleasantly. Never argue with them. Listen to their complaint courteously, but do not encourage them. Don't be distressed by unreasonable complaints. Try to solve these problems as best you can.

- The Angry Guests

  Listen to their complaints, express regret at the occurrence that prompts the complaint. Thank them for calling it to your attention. Try to rectify the error if possible.

- The Troublemakers

  Be courteous, but not be drawn into an argument:
  - Never participate in criticism of the management
  - Never make statements that may be construed as complaints about the restaurant.

The Art of Hosting

50 WAYS TO GAIN GUESTS

1. ALWAYS HAVE A SMILE ON YOUR FACE!!!
2. Make sure table is clean, with no stains or holes
3. Set silverware very straight
4. Make sure that all glassware is spotless
5. Make sure all silverware is perfectly clean
6. Napkins must be clean, with no patches, stains or holes
7. Know house & featured wines thoroughly
8. Pull out chairs and put napkins in laps
9. Acknowledge guests within 30 seconds of arrival
10. Present menu open, holding it from the top
11. Describe daily features at that time
12. Describe them in detail to sound very special
13. Thank the guests once the order has been taken
14. Write food check so anyone can read or serve it
15. Put table & position numbers on checks
16. Serve a basket of bread upon guests' arrival
17. Serve cocktails/wines immediately
18. Set proper silverware **before** serving
19. Serve everything in the proper order
20. Serve food from the left, and clear from the right
21. Serve wines from the right
22. Keep water glasses filled and with ice
23. Refill beverages by lifting by the glass stem
24. Serve ladies first, men last
25. Bring appropriate condiments **with** the meal
26. Offer fresh pepper with all soups, salads, etc.
27. See that there is no wait between courses
28. One server works at a time
29. Always use a dollied underliner for **everything**
30. Always use a tray to carry food/wine/beverages
31. Always know exactly who ordered what
32. Make sure special requests get taken care of

33. Verify that each order is prepared to the guest's specification before leaving the kitchen
34. Ask guests if everything is to their taste
35. Serve hot dishes when they are hot
36. Crumb table after each course
37. Keep table clean and properly maintained
38. Replace dirty ashtray with clean ashtray (never leave more than two cigarette butts in the ashtray)
39. Carry a lighter and use it whenever needed
40. Clear unused table settings
41. Clear butter/bread/condiments before dessert
42. Clear used silverware before next course
43. Clear unused wine glasses after they are finished
44. Clear tray of dirty dishes immediately
45. Have your uniform spotless/starched/ironed
46. Stand straight and **never lean** on anything
47. Put cream/sugar on table **before** serving coffee
48. Coffee cup must be clean inside before pouring
49. Serve regular coffee only if it is fresh (30 min.)
50. Help ladies with chairs when leaving

50 WAYS TO LOSE GUESTS

1. Forget to SMILE
2. Give a grouchy greeting (or none at all!)
3. Let ladies seat themselves
4. Forget to assist ladies in removing their coats
5. Set tables improperly
6. Leave holes or stains in linen
7. Have empty salt/pepper shakers
8. Make guests have to ask for silverware
9. Give guests dirty or bent silverware
10. Give guests chipped glass or china
11. Leave finger marks on plates or glasses
12. Leave coffee spilled in saucers
13. Leave empty sugar bowls on tables
14. Forget garnishes, condiments, etc.
15. Leave an empty bread basket and/or no butter
16. Have dirty ashtrays
17. Forget guests' specific instructions
18. Use a hot plate for cold food
19. Use a cold plate for hot food
20. Touch food or tops of plates with hands
21. Serve from the wrong side
22. Reach in front of guest
23. Don't say, "Pardon", "Sir", or "Madam"
24. Forget who gets what and have to ask
25. Remove plates before all guests are done
26. Don't remove dishes when guests are done
27. Rush guests when they are not in a hurry
28. Don't give guest a new napkin when it felt on the floor
29. Spill things on the floor
30. Scrape crumbs on the floor
31. Leave a littered floor
32. Clatter dishes
33. Leave full trays of dirty dishes in view of guests
34. Ignore guests in another station when they call

35. Have dirty hands or fingernails
36. Have a sloppy or dirty uniform and/or shoes
37. Have body odor, bad breath or too much make-up
38. Smell like a dirty ashtray
39. Chew gum
40. Touch your mouth or nose with your fingers
41. Talk in a group with other servers
42. Talk loudly or argue
43. Bawl out waiters in presence of guests
44. Be too familiar with guests
45. Make a guest wait for his or her check
46. Place the check on the table face up
47. Ask guest to sign the check so you can go home
48. Don't thank your guest
49. Forget to assist guests when leaving
50. Not saying "Good-Bye…"

COMMON WINE TERMINALOGY

AROMA	the perfume coming from the grape (not the smell of a bottle-aged wine)
ASTRINGENT	high tannin content red wine; a drying, mouth-puckering taste, rough and scratchy.
BALANCE	the harmonious relationship between acid, tannin, alcohol and fruit flavors.
BODY	the fruit taste and alcohol strength that give an impression of weight in the mouth.
BOUQUET	the combination of smells attributable to a wine's maturity in the bottle.
BUTTERY	rich, fat character of some Chardonnay produced in a great vintage
BRUT	means "raw" or "bone-dry": the necessarily high acidity of sparkling wines to carry the flavor through the bubbles onto the palate.
CLEAN	a wine with absence of unwanted off odor, taste or color.
CORKY	off taste from a bad cork recognized by a musty-woody smell and flavor in the wine.
CRISP	a pleasing acidy and fresh aftertaste.
DELICATE	the quieter characteristic of an usually light, young and fresh white wine.
DEMI-SEC	French for "half-dry"; half way between "sweet" and "dry"
DECANTING	a process in which the wine contained in the bottle is slowly and carefully poured into a carafe to oxidize the wine and leave sediments inside the bottle.
DRY	a sweet wine that can also be fruity.
ELEGANT	a truly fine, well-balanced wine with finesse.
EARTHY	lower quality wines giving a drying impression in the mouth (comes from grapes grown in heavy clay soils)
FLABBY	too soft, lacking in acidity and without character.

FLINTY	dry, clean, sharp wine (often used to describe French Chablis)
FLOWERY	reminiscent of fresh flowers (typical of many Gewurztraminers)
FRESH	clean, young and lively wine.
FULL	refers to "body" ("full-body"); a wine can be light in body but "full" in flavor.
GRAPY	the taste of fresh grape (often used to describe Beaujolais, Muscat and Riesling)
GRASSY	wines portraying a fresh cut grass or hay smell (used to describe Sauvignon Blanc and certain Gewurztraminer)
GREEN	young, unripe, tart, unbalanced acidity; a youth wine that might improve later.
HARD	a certain severity due to an excess of tannin or acid; can mellow with time.
LIGHT	lack of body, color and alcohol; not a great vintage.
LIQUOREUX	a "liqueur-like" wine often used dessert wines of an unctuous quality.
LIVELY	young fruity wines due to good acidity and a certain carbonic gas content.
MADERIZED	flat and oxidized smell likely due to storage in bright sunlight or too much warmth.
MELLOW	soft, round wine at its peak of maturity.
METHODE CHAMPENOISE	the process of making a second fermentation in the bottle; used in Champagne, France and other good quality sparkling wines.
NOSE	the smell and odor of a wine. Refers to the qualities of aroma and bouquet.
OXIDIZED	1- wines exposed to air, a wine that has lost its freshness. 2- in the bottle it has lost its freshness. For a vintage wine, helping the wine to breathe and deploy its bouquet by the decantation process.
ROBUST	a milder form of aggressive; a big, full wine.

ROUGH	excess tannin in insufficiently aged bottled wines.
ROUND	a wine that has softened the harshness of its tannin through maturity in the bottle.
RUBY	a color resembling the clear red precious stone, as in young red wines.
SEC	French for "dry"; applies to wines without sweetness.
SEDIMENT	tannin and fruit acids that chemically join and fall to the bottom, therefore softening the wine. The decanting process removes the sediments.
SHARP	excessive acidity, whereas bitterness applies to tannin.
SHORT	a wine whose taste quickly disappears after the wine has been swallowed.
SMOOTH	more extreme than "round"
SOFT	mellow taste of the fruit on the palate; if too soft, it implies a weak wine.
SOUND	a well-made wine with no defects.
SOUR	vinegary taste, unfit to drink.
SPARKLING	a wine containing natural or artificial gas: from the addition of SO_2, the addition of sugar that increases the alcohol content and release gas (Chaptalization process), to a double fermentation in a bottle.
SPRITZY	slight effervescence found in some young wines.
SPUMANTE	Italian for "fully sparkling"
STRAW	a pale-golden-colored white wine.
SUBTLE	a wine with significant yet understated characteristics.
SUPPLE	a wine that is easy to drink; not necessarily **soft**, but easier than **round**.
SULFURY	unpleasant rotten egg smell; it comes from the SO_2, an antioxidant with aseptic qualities used in the production of most wines. Noticeable in very young wines, it disappears after a few months or by making a good swirl in the glass or a vigorous decanting to oxidize the wine. If the taste persists, it indicates a faulty wine. Other antioxidants are plaster (used for Port) and resin (used in Greek wines)

SWEET	high residual sugar content.
TANNIN	found in the skin, pip and stalks of the grape and new wooden casks, it is very often used in the "fining" of the wine before fermentation. Its mouth-puckering dryness softens with age to an inky dryness and suppleness.
TART	sharpness due to high noticeable acidity.
TASTEVIN	a shallow, dimpled, silver cup used for tasting wines. The sommelier usually has one around his neck.
THIN	lacking in body and alcohol; watery and will not improve with age.
VELVETY	soft mouth feel with a silky texture.
VERMOUTH	an aromatized wine. (Origin "wermut", German for wormwood, its principal ingredient)
VINTAGE	a wine of one year's harvest only; may be anything from poor to exceptional: a vintage wine does not indicate a wine of a special quality
WOODY	excessive wood odor and/or flavor.
YEASTY	not complimentary for most wines, but a **yeasty bouquet** is desirable in many sparkling wines.

THE TEN COMMANDMENTS

I

The Guest is the most important person in our business.

II

The Guest is not dependent on us – we are dependent on him.

III

The Guest is not an interruption of our work; he is the purpose of it.

IV

The Guest is part of our business, not an outsider.

V

The Guest is the lifeblood of the business, just as you are.

VI

The Guest brings us his desires; it is our job to fulfill them.

VII

The Guest is a human being with feelings and emotions.

VII

The Guest is someone to be welcomed warmly and graciously.

IX

The Guest is deserving of the most courtesy and attention possible.

X

The Guest pays our salary.

Index